SILVER EDITION

Mosaic 2

ACADEMIC ESSAY DEVELOPMENT **WRITING**

Laurie Blass
Meredith Pike-Baky

Lawrence J. Zwier
Contributor, Focus on Testing

Meredith Pike-Baky
Writing Strand Leader

Mosaic 2 Writing, Silver Edition

Published by McGraw-Hill ESL/ELT, a business unit of The McGraw-Hill Companies, Inc., 1221 Avenue of the Americas, New York, NY 10020.

ISBN 13: 978-0-07-325184-4 (Student Book)
ISBN 10: 0-07-325184-4
1 2 3 4 5 6 7 8 9 10 VNH 11 10 09 08 07 06

Editorial director: Erik Gundersen
Series editor: Valerie Kelemen
Developmental editor: Amy Lawler
Production manager: Juanita Thompson
Production coordinators: Vanessa Nuttry, James D. Gwyn
Cover designer: Robin Locke Monda
Interior designer: Nesbitt Graphics, Inc.
Photo researcher: Photoquick Research

The credits section for this book begins on page 195 and is considered an extension of the copyright page.

Cover photo: Jeffery Becom/Lonely Planet

A Special Thank You

The Interactions/Mosaic Silver Edition team wishes to thank our extended team: teachers, students, administrators, and teacher trainers, all of whom contributed invaluably to the making of this edition.

Macarena Aguilar, **North Harris College**, Houston, Texas ■ Mohamad Al-Alam, **Imam Mohammad University**, Riyadh, Saudi Arabia ■ Faisal M. Al Mohanna Abaalkhail, **King Saud University**, Riyadh, Saudi Arabia; Amal Al-Toaimy, **Women's College, Prince Sultan University**, Riyadh, Saudi Arabia ■ Douglas Arroliga, **Ave Maria University**, Managua, Nicaragua ■ Fairlie Atkinson, **Sungkyunkwan University**, Seoul, Korea ■ Jose R. Bahamonde, **Miami-Dade Community College**, Miami, Florida ■ John Ball, **Universidad de las Americas**, Mexico City, Mexico ■ Steven Bell, **Universidad la Salle**, Mexico City, Mexico ■ Damian Benstead, **Sungkyunkwan University**, Seoul, Korea ■ Paul Cameron, **National Chengchi University**, Taipei, Taiwan R.O.C. ■ Sun Chang, **Soongsil University**, Seoul, Korea ■ Grace Chao, **Soochow University**, Taipei, Taiwan R.O.C. ■ Chien Ping Chen, **Hua Fan University**, Taipei, Taiwan R.O.C. ■ Selma Chen, **Chihlee Institute of Technology**, Taipei, Taiwan R.O.C. ■ Sylvia Chiu, **Soochow University**, Taipei, Taiwan R.O.C. ■ Mary Colonna, **Columbia University**, New York, New York ■ Lee Culver, **Miami-Dade Community College**, Miami, Florida ■ Joy Durighello, **City College of San Francisco**, San Francisco, California ■ Isabel Del Valle, **ULATINA**, San Jose, Costa Rica ■ Linda Emerson, **Sogang University**, Seoul, Korea ■ Esther Entin, **Miami-Dade Community College**, Miami, Florida ■ Glenn Farrier, **Gakushuin Women's College**, Tokyo, Japan ■ Su Wei Feng, Taipei, Taiwan R.O.C. ■ Judith Garcia, **Miami-Dade Community College**, Miami, Florida ■ Maxine Gillway, **United Arab Emirates University**, Al Ain, United Arab Emirates ■ Colin Gullberg, **Soochow University**, Taipei, Taiwan R.O.C. ■ Natasha Haugnes, **Academy of Art University**, San Francisco, California ■ Barbara Hockman, **City College of San Francisco**, San Francisco, California ■ Jinyoung Hong, **Sogang University**, Seoul, Korea ■ Sherry Hsieh, **Christ's College**, Taipei, Taiwan R.O.C. ■ Yu-shen Hsu, **Soochow University**, Taipei, Taiwan R.O.C. ■ Cheung Kai-Chong, **Shih-Shin University**, Taipei, Taiwan R.O.C. ■ Leslie Kanberg, **City College of San Francisco**, San Francisco, California ■ Gregory Keech, **City College of San Francisco**, San Francisco, California ■ Susan Kelly, **Sogang University**, Seoul, Korea ■ Myoungsuk Kim, **Soongsil University**, Seoul, Korea ■ Youngsuk Kim, **Soongsil University**, Seoul, Korea ■ Roy Langdon, **Sungkyunkwan University**, Seoul, Korea ■ Rocio Lara, **University of Costa Rica**, San Jose, Costa Rica ■ Insung Lee, **Soongsil University**, Seoul, Korea ■ Andy Leung, **National Tsing Hua University**, Taipei, Taiwan R.O.C. ■ Elisa Li Chan, **University of Costa Rica**, San Jose, Costa Rica ■ Elizabeth Lorenzo, **Universidad Internacional de las Americas**, San Jose, Costa Rica ■ Cheryl Magnant, **Sungkyunkwan University**, Seoul, Korea ■ Narciso Maldonado Iuit, **Escuela Tecnica Electricista**, Mexico City, Mexico ■ Shaun Manning, **Hankuk University of Foreign Studies**, Seoul, Korea ■ Yoshiko Matsubayashi, **Tokyo International University**, Saitama, Japan ■ Scott Miles, **Sogang University**, Seoul, Korea ■ William Mooney, **Chinese Culture University**, Taipei, Taiwan R.O.C. ■ Jeff Moore, **Sungkyunkwan University**, Seoul, Korea ■ Mavelin de Moreno, **Lehnsen Roosevelt School**, Guatemala City, Guatemala ■ Ahmed Motala, **University of Sharjah**, Sharjah, United Arab Emirates ■ Carlos Navarro, **University of Costa Rica**, San Jose, Costa Rica ■ Dan Neal, **Chih Chien University**, Taipei, Taiwan R.O.C. ■ Margarita Novo, **University of Costa Rica**, San Jose, Costa Rica ■ Karen O'Neill, **San Jose State University**, San Jose, California ■ Linda O'Roke, **City College of San Francisco**, San Francisco, California ■ Martha Padilla, **Colegio de Bachilleres de Sinaloa,** Culiacan, Mexico ■ Allen Quesada, **University of Costa Rica**, San Jose, Costa Rica ■ Jim Rogge, **Broward Community College**, Ft. Lauderdale, Florida ■ Marge Ryder, **City College of San Francisco**, San Francisco, California ■ Gerardo Salas, **University of Costa Rica**, San Jose, Costa Rica ■ Shigeo Sato, **Tamagawa University**, Tokyo, Japan ■ Lynn Schneider, **City College of San Francisco**, San Francisco, California ■ Devan Scoble, **Sungkyunkwan University**, Seoul, Korea ■ Maryjane Scott, **Soongsil University**, Seoul, Korea ■ Ghaida Shaban, **Makassed Philanthropic School**, Beirut, Lebanon ■ Maha Shalok, **Makassed Philanthropic School**, Beirut, Lebanon ■ John Shannon, **University of Sharjah**, Sharjah, United Arab Emirates ■ Elsa Sheng, **National Technology College of Taipei**, Taipei, Taiwan R.O.C. ■ Ye-Wei Sheng, **National Taipei College of Business**, Taipei, Taiwan R.O.C. ■ Emilia Sobaja, **University of Costa Rica**, San Jose, Costa Rica ■ You-Souk Yoon, **Sungkyunkwan University**, Seoul, Korea ■ Shanda Stromfield, **San Jose State University**, San Jose, California ■ Richard Swingle, **Kansai Gaidai College**, Osaka, Japan ■ Carol Sung, **Christ's College**, Taipei, Taiwan R.O.C. ■ Jeng-Yih Tim Hsu, **National Kaohsiung First University of Science and Technology**, Kaohsiung, Taiwan R.O.C. ■ Shinichiro Torikai, **Rikkyo University**, Tokyo, Japan ■ Sungsoon Wang, **Sogang University**, Seoul, Korea ■ Kathleen Wolf, **City College of San Francisco**, San Francisco, California ■ Sean Wray, **Waseda University International**, Tokyo, Japan ■ Belinda Yanda, **Academy of Art University**, San Francisco, California ■ Su Huei Yang, **National Taipei College of Business**, Taipei, Taiwan R.O.C. ■ Tzu Yun Yu, **Chungyu Institute of Technology**, Taipei, Taiwan R.O.C.

Author Acknowledgements

Grateful acknowledgements to: Erik Gundersen, Valerie Kelemen, Amy Lawler, Jennifer Wilson, Mari Vargo, and strand leaders Pam Hartmann and Jami Hanreddy.

To Nick, Alex, and Sarah who grew up alongside Mosaic and have become more helpful, thoughtful, and more gratifying — just like the Silver Edition.

Table of Contents

Welcome to Interactions/Mosaic Silver Edition

Interactions/Mosaic **Silver Edition** is a fully-integrated, 18-book academic skills series. Language proficiencies are articulated from the beginning through advanced levels within each of the four language skill strands. Chapter themes articulate across the four skill strands to systematically recycle content, vocabulary, and grammar.

NEW to the Silver Edition:

- **World's most popular and comprehensive academic skills series**—thoroughly updated for today's global learners
- **New design** showcases compelling instructional photos to strengthen the educational experience
- **Enhanced focus on vocabulary building, test taking, and critical thinking skills** promotes academic achievement
- **New strategies and activities for the TOEFL®iBT** build invaluable test taking skills
- **New "Best Practices" approach** promotes excellence in language teaching

NEW to Mosaic 2 Writing:

- **All new content:**—Chapter 4 Beauty and Aesthetics
- **Transparent chapter structure** with consistent part headings, activity labeling, and clear guidance—strengthens the academic experience:

  Part 1: Preparing to Write
  Part 2: Focusing on Words and Phrases
  Part 3: Organizing and Developing Your Ideas
  Part 4: Evaluating Your Writing

- **Writing Articulation Chart** (inside back cover) shows how the four Writing books lead students from successful sentence building to effective academic essay writing
- **Systematically structured, multi-step *Writing Process*** culminates in a *Writing Product* task
- **New communicative activities** invite students to interact meaningfully with target words to build vocabulary skills for writing
- **New self-evaluation rubric** for each chapter supports the learner as he or she builds confidence and autonomy in academic writing

---

* TOEFL is a registered trademark of Educational Testing Service (ETS). This publication is not endorsed or approved by ETS.

Interactions/Mosaic Best Practices

Our Interactions/Mosaic Silver Edition team has produced an edition that focuses on Best Practices, principles that contribute to excellent language teaching and learning. Our team of writers, editors, and teacher consultants has identified the following six interconnected Best Practices:

Making Use of Academic Content

Materials and tasks based on academic content and experiences give learning real purpose. Students explore real world issues, discuss academic topics, and study content-based and thematic materials.

Organizing Information

Students learn to organize thoughts and notes through a variety of graphic organizers that accommodate diverse learning and thinking styles.

Scaffolding Instruction

A scaffold is a physical structure that facilitates construction of a building. Similarly, scaffolding instruction is a tool used to facilitate language learning in the form of predictable and flexible tasks. Some examples include oral or written modeling by the teacher or students, placing information in a larger framework, and reinterpretation.

Activating Prior Knowledge

Students can better understand new spoken or written material when they connect to the content. Activating prior knowledge allows students to tap into what they already know, building on this knowledge, and stirring a curiosity for more knowledge.

Interacting with Others

Activities that promote human interaction in pair work, small group work, and whole class activities present opportunities for real world contact and real world use of language.

Cultivating Critical Thinking

Strategies for critical thinking are taught explicitly. Students learn tools that promote critical thinking skills crucial to success in the academic world.

Highlights of Mosaic 2 Writing Silver Edition

Interacting with Others
Questions and topical quotes stimulate interest, activate prior knowledge, and launch the topic of the unit.

Activating Prior Knowledge
Chapter opening questions and pre-writing discussions activate prior knowledge and create a foundation for the writing activity.

Chapter 4

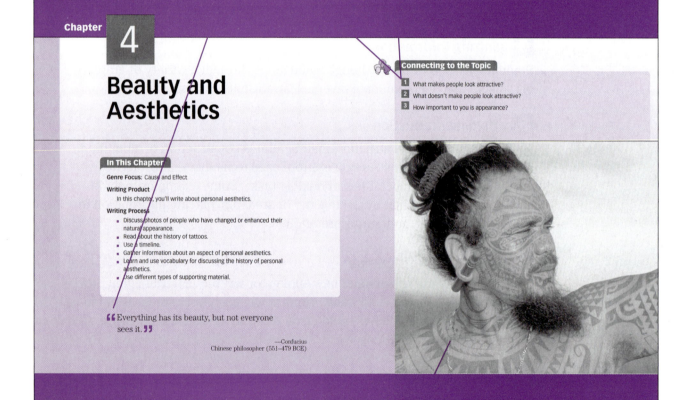

Beauty and Aesthetics

Connecting to the Topic

1. What makes people look attractive?
2. What doesn't make people look attractive?
3. How important to you is appearance?

In This Chapter

Genre Focus: Cause and Effect

Writing Product
In this chapter, you'll write about personal aesthetics.

Writing Process
- Discuss photos of people who have changed or enhanced their natural appearance.
- Read about the history of tattoos.
- Use a timeline.
- Gather information about an aspect of personal aesthetics.
- Learn and use vocabulary for discussing the history of personal aesthetics.
- Use different types of supporting material.

"Everything has its beauty, but not everyone sees it."

—Confucius
Chinese philosopher (551–479 BCE)

New design showcases compelling instructional photos to strengthen the educational experience.

Making Use of Academic Content
Academic themes, activities, and writing topics prepare students for university life.

Organizing Information
Graphic organizers provide tools for organizing information and ideas.

Part 1 Preparing to Write

Getting Started

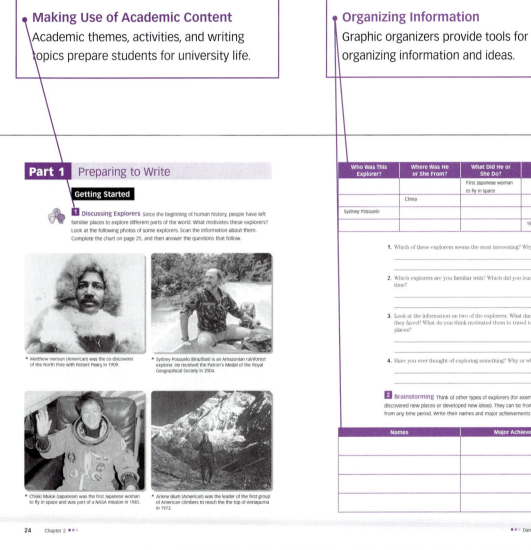

1 Discussing Explorers Since the beginning of human history, people have left familiar places to explore different parts of the world. What motivates these explorers? Look at the following photos of some explorers. Scan the information about them. Complete the chart on page 25, and then answer the questions that follow.

Matthew Henson (American) was the co-discoverer of the North Pole with Robert Peary in 1909.

Sydney Possuelo (Brazilian) is an Amazonian rainforest explorer. He received the Patron's Medal of the Royal Geographical Society in 2004.

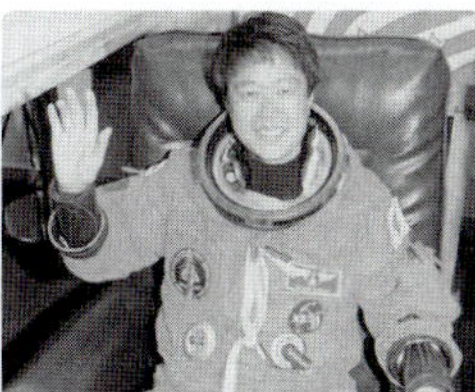

Chiaki Mukai (Japanese) was the first Japanese woman to fly in space and was part of a NASA mission in 1985.

Arlene Blum (American) was the leader of the first group of American climbers to reach the the top of Annapurna in 1972.

Who Was This Explorer?	Where Was He or She From?	What Did He or She Do?	When Did He or She Do It?
		First Japanese woman to fly in space	
	China		
Sydney Possuelo			
			1972

1. Which of these explorers seems the most interesting? Why?
2. Which explorers are you familiar with? Which did you learn about for the first time?
3. Look at the information on two of the explorers. What dangers do you think they faced? What do you think motivated them to travel to the unfamiliar places?
4. Have you ever thought of exploring something? Why or why not?

2 Brainstorming Think of other types of explorers (for example, people who discovered new places or developed new ideas). They can be from any country and from any time period. Write their names and major achievements in the chart below.

Names	Major Achievements

Cultivating Critical Thinking

Critical thinking strategies and activities equip students with the skills they need for academic achievement.

Enhanced focus on vocabulary building

Enhanced focus on vocabulary building promotes academic achievement.

Strategy

Thinking Critically: ***Recognizing Supporting Information from Experts***

Experts are people with special qualifications in a particular field. Writers often give examples, descriptions, and explanations from experts to support their main ideas. This helps the reader to understand the author's ideas, and it also makes them seem more valid (true®because other people have done research to prove them.

5 Finding Supporting Information Who are the experts that the author of "Gender Differences in Communication" uses to support the idea that men and women have different communication styles? Complete the following chart with their names, their qualifications, and an example of their findings.

Name	Qualifications	Findings
Jennifer Coates		
	Wrote *He Says, She Says: Closing the Communication Gap Between the Sexes*	.
		Men are more assertive than women are on discussion boards.
Gladys We		

6 Freewriting Write on the topic below for 15 minutes without stopping.

Think of problems that you have had communicating with the opposite sex. Describe one or more situations in which you have misunderstood or been misunderstood by a member of the opposite sex.

7 Gathering Information Collect examples of the differences between male and female communication styles. Look for examples by watching movies, plays, or TV shows that feature male-female relationships; or by watching people in public places such as school, work, or a restaurant. Look for the differences described in the article "Gender Differences in Communication" as well as for others, such as interrupting, body language, word choice, conversation topic choice, boasting/bragging, or swearing. Take notes on the differences that you notice.

▲ An example of different communication styles

50 Chapter 3

8 Sharing Results In small groups, report on the examples of male and female communication style differences that you observed in your research. If possible, illustrate the differences you found by reenacting a scene from a movie, TV show, or play that you saw.

Part 2 Focusing on Words and Phrases

Discussing Communication Differences

1 Finding Meaning in Context Here are some words and expressions from "Gender Differences in Communication" on pages 48–49. Find them in the passage. Notice their contexts—how they are used in a sentence—and try to guess their meanings. Then match the meanings on the right to the words and expressions on the left. Write the letters on the lines.

Words and Expressions	Meanings
____ **1.** anonymous (Line 49®	**a.** different
____ **2.** assertive (Line 38®	**b.** ways of speaking
____ **3.** associated with (Line 7®	**c.** related to or caused by
____ **4.** dominate (Line 22®	**d.** connect with; interact with another person
____ **5.** empathy (Line 13®	**e.** having an understanding with another person; mutual understanding
____ **6.** findings (Line 25®	**f.** closeness
____ **7.** intimacy (Line 12®	**g.** feeling what another person feels
____ **8.** liberating (Line 49®	**h.** stay with
____ **9.** rapport (Line 9®	**i.** have control or power over
____ **10.** relate (Line 9®	**j.** results of research
____ **11.** speech characteristics (Line 6®	**k.** speaking with confidence
____ **12.** stick to (Line 17®	**l.** freeing
____ **13.** varying (Line 5®	**m.** unknown; not named

Gender and Relationships 51

Scaffolding Instruction
Instruction and practice with sentence and paragraph skills help build a solid foundation for essay writing.

New strategies and activities for the TOEFL®iBT build invaluable test taking skills.

5 Writing Thesis Statements The following are sets of notes on topics related to explorers and exploring. Read the notes and then write a good thesis statement for each set below.

et 1
Jacques Cousteau
- *Born in France in 1910*
- *Undersea explorer*
- *Helped invent the aqualung, which enables people to breathe underwater*
- *Wrote The Silent World*
- *Perfected watertight movie cameras*
- *alvaged cargo from many sunken ships underwater*
- *Made many films*
- *Invented the bathyscaphe, which enables observation two miles below the surface of the water*

et 2
Dangers in pace
- *People in space are totally dependent on their vehicle.*
- *Meteors can tear holes in spaceships.*
- *Cosmic rays could be a threat.*
- *If people travel far from Earth, certain kinds of radiation could be harmful.*
- *Ultraviolet rays could cause burns.*

Cousteau
____
____
____

Dangers in pace
____
____
____

TOEFL® IBT

Focus on Testing

Writing Thesis Statements

You just learned about writing a good thesis statement. This is especially challenging on the TOEFL iBT test, which gives you very little time to plan, write, and review your responses. Time that you would ordinarily spend in carefully deciding on a thesis statement is simply not available under TOEFL iBT conditions. This means that you have to compose a strong thesis statement quickly and without a lot of thought.

The best way to find the basis for a thesis statement is to look carefully at the prompt. It contains ideas, and even phrases, that can guide you to a relevant and meaningful thesis statement.

Practice Read the following sample prompts. Identify and underline parts of each prompt that could be paraphrased to make a good thesis statement. Then write a thesis statement for a response. The first two are done for you as examples.

1. **Prompt:** Because accidents have been increasing, the university is considering closing many roads to cars. Only foot traffic and bicyclists would be allowed on these roads. Do you think this is a good idea or not?

   Sample thesis statement: Keeping cars off many university roads would definitely reduce the number of accidents on campus.

2. **Prompt:** Using information from both the reading and the lecture, explain the goals of the U.S. Social Security system.

   Sample thesis statement: Both the reading and the lecture point out that the Social Security system in the U.S. aims to provide basic financial support for retired persons and for disabled workers.

   Note: In this situation, certain phrases (e.g., *Social Security system*) from the prompt should be directly borrowed because there is no convenient way to paraphrase them.

Scope and Sequence

Chapter	Writing Product	Preparing to Write	Focusing on Words and Phrases
1 Languages and Learning page 2	■ A **descriptive** essay on the best way to learn a foreign language	■ Discussing second and foreign languages ■ Interviewing ■ Reading: *Want to Learn a Language? Don't Make It a Mount Everest* ■ Freewriting ■ Gathering information: Interview	■ Recognizing idioms ■ Words and phrases for describing foreign language learning
2 Danger and Daring page 22	■ An **informational** essay about an explorer	■ Discussing explorers ■ Brainstorming ■ Reading: *Annapurna*: *A Woman's Place* ■ Freewriting ■ Gathering information	■ Words and phrases for describing explorers ■ Expressions for describing personalities and achievements of explorers
3 Gender and Relationships page 44	■ A **descriptive** essay comparing communication style differences between men and women	■ Discussing gender communication styles ■ Brainstorming ■ Reading: *Gender Differences in Communication* ■ Freewriting ■ Gathering information: Recording observations	■ Words and phrases for discussing communication differences ■ Words and phrases for showing similarities and differences

Organizing and Developing Your Ideas	Critical Thinking	Focus on Testing	Evaluating Your Writing
■ Essay form and function ■ Discovering the academic essay	■ Interpreting images ■ Using a graphic organizer to visualize main ideas and details ■ Recognizing cultural references ■ Analyzing an academic essay	TOEFL® IBT ■ Checking your responses	■ Rubric for writing about learning a new language ■ Self-assessment log
■ The thesis statement: Topic and approach ■ Supporting ideas	■ Interpreting images ■ Using a graphic organizer to visualize main ideas and details ■ Making predictions ■ Analyzing thesis statements and supporting ideas ■ Making predictions from thesis statements	TOEFL® IBT ■ Writing thesis statements	■ Rubric for writing about an explorer ■ Self-assessment log
■ Paragraph development ■ Anticipating readers' questions	■ Interpreting images ■ Recognizing supporting information from experts ■ Analyzing and evaluating paragraphs	TOEFL® IBT ■ Pretending that you are the reader	■ Rubric for writing about gender differences in communication ■ Self-assessment log

Chapter	Writing Product	Preparing to Write	Focusing on Words and Phrases
4 Beauty and Aesthetics page 60	■ A **cause and effect** essay on an aspect of personal aesthetics	■ Discussing personal aesthetics ■ Identifying personal choices ■ Reading: *Tattoos Across Time and Place* ■ Freewriting ■ Gathering information: Library and Internet research	■ Words and phrases for discussing the history of personal aesthetics
5 Transitions page 80	■ An **informational** essay that describes and analyzes a rite of passage	■ Discussing rites of passages ■ Brainstorming ■ Reading: *The Life Course* ■ Freewriting ■ Gathering information: Interview	■ Words and phrases for discussing rites of passage
6 The Mind page 98	■ An **analysis** essay that describes and interprets a dream	■ Discussing dreams ■ Interviewing ■ Reading: *The Dream That Haunts You* ■ Freewriting ■ Gathering information: Library and Internet research	■ Words and phrases for interpreting dreams

Organizing and Developing Your Ideas	Critical Thinking	Focus on Testing	Evaluating Your Writing
■ Types of supporting material ■ Identifying types of supporting material ■ Organizing supporting material	■ Interpreting images ■ Using a timeline ■ Analyzing examples of supporting material ■ Using a graphic organizer to categorize supporting material	TOEFL® IBT ■ Examples, details, and reasons	■ Rubric for writing about personal aesthetics ■ Self-assessment log
■ Organizing supporting material ■ Interpreting supporting material	■ Interpreting images ■ Interpreting tables ■ Analyzing a well-developed paragraph ■ Analyzing an interpretation paragraph	TOEFL® IBT ■ Writing about personal transitions on standardized tests	■ Rubric for writing about a rite of passage ■ Self-assessment log
■ Paragraph organization: Levels of generality ■ Paragraph patterns: Top-Down organization and divided organization	■ Interpreting images ■ Interpreting symbols ■ Using a graphic organizer to interpret symbols ■ Analyzing divided organization ■ Analyzing levels of generality	TOEFL® IBT ■ "Drawing" your ideas for TOEFL iBT® writing	■ Rubric for writing about a dream ■ Self-assessment log

Chapter	Writing Product	Preparing to Write	Focusing on Words and Phrases
7 Working page 118	▪ An **analysis** essay on the qualities that contribute to success at work	▪ Discussing work ▪ Taking a quiz ▪ Reading: *Decision by Consensus* ▪ Freewriting ▪ Gathering information: Interview	▪ Words and phrases for describing work in a multicultural setting ▪ Expressions for introducing cause and effect
8 Breakthroughs page 136	▪ A **definition** essay that describes an important energy conservation development	▪ Discussing solar power ▪ Discussing advantages and disadvantages ▪ Reading: *Spray-On Solar-Power Cells Are True Breakthrough* ▪ Freewriting ▪ Gathering information: presenting research	▪ Words and phrases for discussing energy ▪ Words and expressions for describing technology
9 Art and Entertainment page 152	▪ An **interpretation** essay that describes a work of art and what it says about the artist or the artist's culture	▪ Discussing works of art ▪ Brainstorming ▪ Reading: *Themes and Purposes of Art*: Art and Nature ▪ Freewriting ▪ Gathering information: Library and Internet research	▪ Words and phrases for describing and analyzing art
10 Conflict and Reconciliation page 168	▪ An **argument** essay that explains a problem and presents one or more solutions	▪ Discussing conflicts and solutions ▪ Reading: *Turtle Island (Selections)* ▪ Freewriting	▪ Words and phrases for discussing problems and solutions

Organizing and Developing Your Ideas	Critical Thinking	Focus on Testing	Evaluating Your Writing
■ Cause and effect ■ Causal relationships: Analyzing causes and effects ■ Casual chain essay organization I ■ Causal chain essay organization II	■ Interpreting images ■ Using a graphic organizer to compare and contrast ■ Making inferences ■ Using a graphic organizer to summarize advantages and disadvantages ■ Using a graphic organizer to show causal relationships	TOEFL® IBT ■ Having a repertoire of organizational patterns	■ Rubric for writing about qualities that contribute to success at work ■ Self-assessment log
■ Describing processes ■ Process paragraphs	■ Interpreting images ■ Using a graphic organizer to summarize advantages and disadvantages ■ Expanding the literal meanings of words	TOEFL® IBT ■ Listing signals in writing for standardized tests	■ Rubric for describing an important energy conservation development ■ Self-assessment log
■ Writing introductions ■ Writing conclusions	■ Interpreting images ■ Using a graphic organizer to make comparisons ■ Applying what you've learned	TOEFL® IBT ■ Having a repertoire of introductions and conclusions	■ Rubric for describing a work of art ■ Self-assessment log
■ Discussing problems and solutions	■ Interpreting images ■ Interpreting metaphors ■ Using a graphic organizer to analyze sides of an issue and solutions ■ Using consensus to solve a problem ■ Analyzing a problem-solution thesis statement	TOEFL® IBT ■ Brainstorming to get started	■ Rubric for writing about a problem and one or more solutions ■ Self-assessment log

Chapter 1

Languages and Learning

In This Chapter

Genre Focus: Descriptive

Writing Product

In this chapter, you'll write about learning a language.

Writing Process

- Discuss photos of people speaking a second language.
- Read about learning a second language.
- Recognize cultural references.
- Interview people about their language-learning experiences.
- Learn and use vocabulary for writing about language learning.
- Discover essay form and function.
- Write and evaluate an essay.

"To have another language is to possess a second soul."

—Charlemagne
Frankish king (742–814)

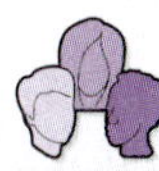

Connecting to the Topic

1. What are some reasons to learn a second language?
2. What are some ways to learn a second language?
3. What are some places you might go to learn a second language?

Part 1 Preparing to Write

Getting Started

1 Discussing Second and Foreign Languages What are the advantages of learning a second language? Look at the photos and answer the questions that follow.

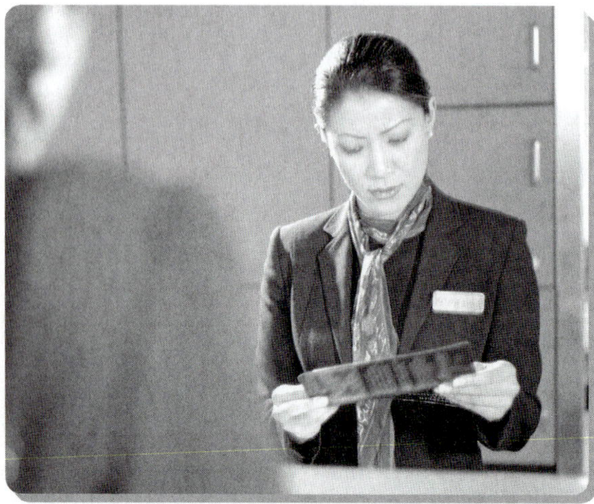

▲ 1. An airline representative

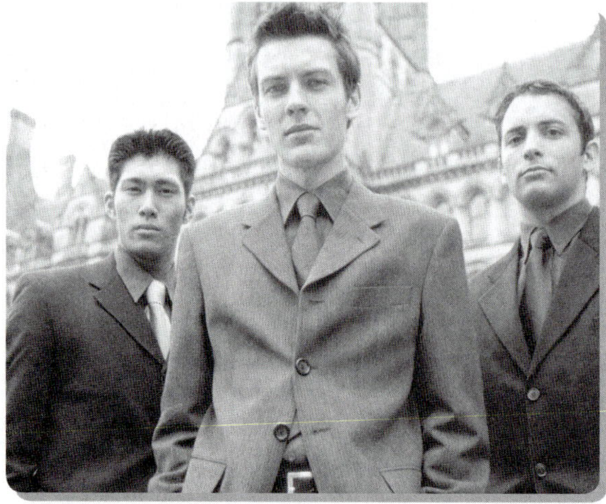

▲ 2. Doing business in a foreign country

▲ 3. Studying in a foreign country

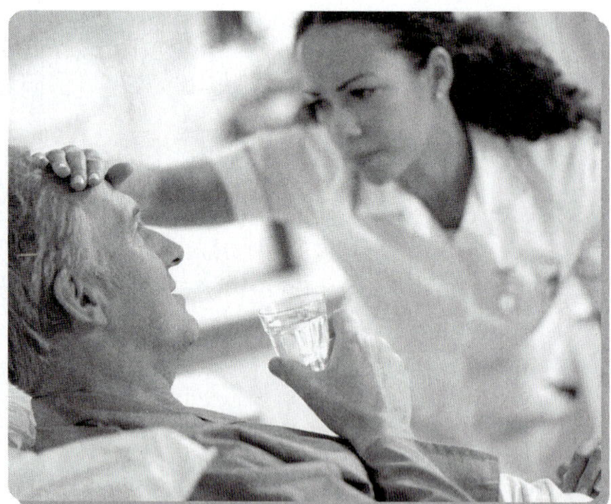

▲ 4. Working in a health clinic

1. Why might these people need to speak more than one language?

____

____

2. What are some other reasons to learn a second or foreign language?

____

____

3. What are some ways to learn a second or foreign language?

____

____

2 Interviewing Interview a classmate about his or her language-learning experiences. Use the following questionnaire and add your own questions, if you wish.

Questionnaire

1. How many languages do you know? _______________________

2. Rate your ability in your second language(s):

Foreign language 1: _______________________

(Circle the appropriate number.) 1 poor 2 3 4 5 6 excellent

Foreign language 2: _______________________

(Circle the appropriate number.) 1 poor 2 3 4 5 6 excellent

Foreign language 3: _______________________

(Circle the appropriate number.) 1 poor 2 3 4 5 6 excellent

3. Think about the foreign language that you are the most fluent in. How did you learn it (for example, in school, while traveling, working, studying in the country, or a combination)?

____

____

____

4. Did a teacher help you learn? How much?

____

____

____

(continued on the next page)

5. Could you have learned the language without a teacher? Explain.

____

____

____

6. What else helped you learn this language (books, tutors, classmates, a computer program, the language itself was easy to learn, native speakers were helpful or friendly)?

____

____

____

7. What strategies did you use while you were learning this language? Examples of strategies are:

- Having conversations with lots of different people
- Keeping a notebook with you at all times
- Asking native speakers for help
- Making flashcards
- Watching TV with captions turned on

____

____

____

____

3 Preparing to Read On the next page is an article from the *New York Times* about learning a new language. Before you read it, answer the questions below.

1. In your opinion, what makes a good language learner?

____

____

2. What makes a good language teacher?

____

____

3. What's the best way to learn a new language? In a class? On your own? What types of materials are best? How long should a language course last? What else is important?

____

____

Want to Learn a Language? Don't Make It a Mount Everest

A It's common to see and hear foreign languages every day in New York City: riding with Creole-speaking cabdrivers, reading menus written half in Chinese and half in Spanish, or making midnight purchases in Korean-owned delicatessens.

B Learning them, on the other hand, is another matter and it almost always costs money. Finding a bargain in learning any language is rare, even though the Manhattan *Yellow Pages* alone list some 70 foreign language schools.

C Experts in the field of foreign language teaching say that if you want to become a polyglot, you should consider several things before you sign up for a language course:

Motive

D Why do you need to learn a foreign language? Being able to order a drink on the French island of Martinique is very different from doing business in Tokyo. Or, if all you want to know is how to find a telephone booth while walking near the Arc de Triomphe in Paris, a practical program in which you first learn to speak, and later to read and write, would do fine.

▲ Studying English in a language lab

E "In this age of global travel, it is increasingly likely that students have spent time or will spend time in the country of the language that they want to learn," said Anthony Niesz, associate director of the Yale University Language Laboratory. This means that knowing how to ask for a hotel room or for directions—and to understand the answer you receive—is more important than being able to read a newspaper like *Le Monde*, or even knowing the pluperfect tense.

F But if real proficiency is your goal—from being able to conjugate verbs to reading *Madame Bovary* in French—a university or an institute may be the best place for you.

Method

G What's the best way to learn a language? Language teaching programs and methods vary. One technique is called *total immersion.* With total immersion, students in the classroom speak, listen to, and read only the foreign language they are learning. And for some, total immersion is the closest thing to learning a language while living in the foreign country.

H Since most programs emphasize dialogue in the classroom, class size is crucial. If there are more than 15 students, individuals are likely to spend too much time silent, Mr. Niesz said. The experts, however, say smaller and more expensive classes are not necessarily better.

I For serious students who don't have a lot of time, private tutoring may be best. But groups work well for most people because they provide the opportunity to participate in games, skits, and conversation.

Teacher

J What makes a good teacher? When you consider a language class, you must, of course, consider the teacher. Learning a language from native speakers has its advantages, but "being a native speaker is no guarantee that a person will be a good teacher," Mr. Niesz said. He added, "By far the most important criterion is whether he or she is an enthusiastic teacher."

K Phyllis Ziegler, the director of second-language programs for the New York Public Schools' division of bilingual education, said that "the non-native teacher may sometimes better understand the student's questions because he or she has also studied the target language."

L So, before inquiring about the authenticity of the teacher's accent, ask about educational experience and credentials.

M Fabio Girelli-Carasi, the director of foreign languages at New York University's School of Continuing Education, said that "the tanning-booth approach to language doesn't work." He added, "Just sitting there ten hours won't make you darker than five." In other words, do your homework.

—Adapted from an article by Tish Durkin, *The New York Times*

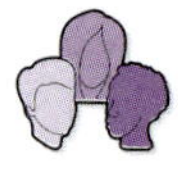

4 Understanding the Reading In small groups, answer these questions:

1. What three things should you consider before you sign up for a language course?

   ____

2. Do you agree with this article? Why or why not?

   ____

   ____

   ____

3. What are your motives for learning English? Complete this sentence: "I need to/want to learn English in order to . . ." Be as specific as possible. Then share your answer with a partner.

____

____

Strategy

Using a Graphic Organizer

A graphic organizer is a kind of chart. It can help you visualize the main ideas and the details in a reading. It can also help you visualize connections between ideas. In Activity 5, you will use a graphic organizer to organize ideas from the article you read above. First, in the boxes on the left, list what a student should consider before signing up for a language course. Then, in the boxes on the right, give examples for each consideration.

5 Completing a Graphic Organizer Complete the following graphic organizer with ideas from the article "Want to Learn a Language? Don't Make It a Mount Everest."

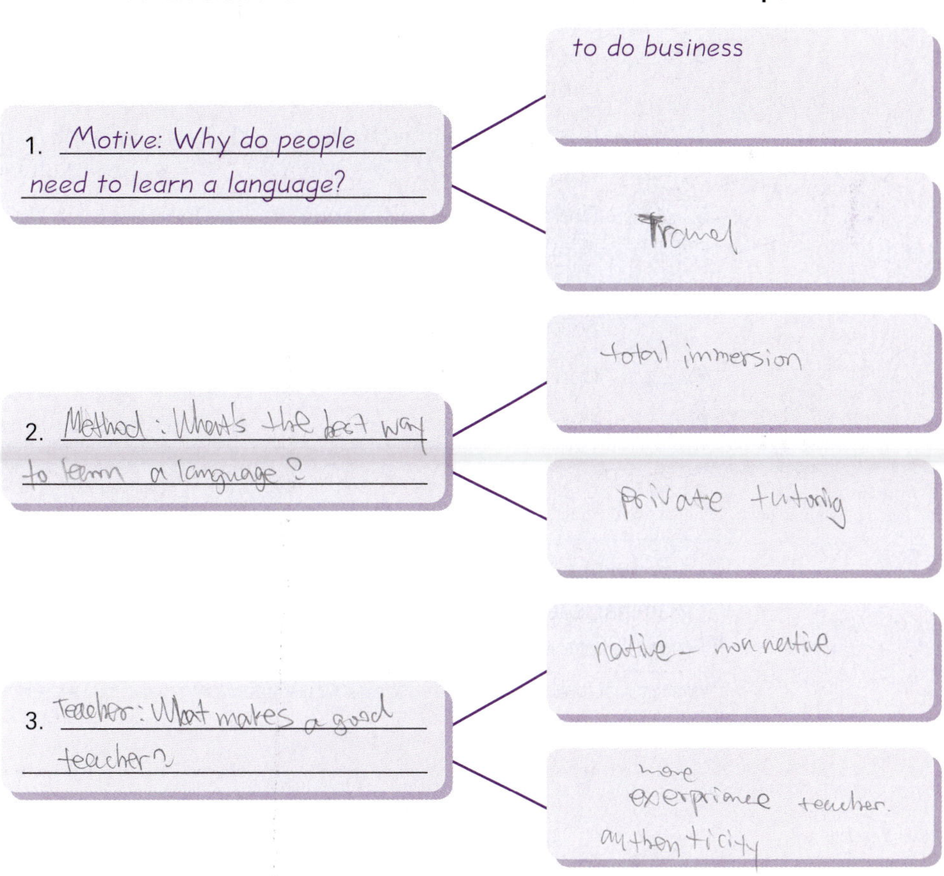

Considerations
Examples
to do business
1. Motive: Why do people need to learn a language?
Travel
total immersion
2. Method: What's the best way to learn a language?
private tutoring
native – non native
3. Teacher: What makes a good teacher?
authenticity

Strategy

Thinking Critically: *Recognizing Cultural References*

To get and keep the reader's attention, magazine and newspaper writers often use puns, idioms, proverbs, and other words and expressions that people in the same culture recognize. These are called *cultural references*. Recognizing and understanding these references is an important critical thinking skill.

An example is the title of the article that you just read: "Want to Learn a Language? Don't Make It a Mount Everest." It comes from a North American English idiom: "Don't make a mountain out of a molehill" (A molehill is a small pile of dirt). It means: "Don't turn a small or easy job into a difficult one."

6 Recognizing Idioms Below are some more idioms. How many do you know? Match the meaning with the idiom. Write the letters on the lines.

1. ____ Don't look a gift horse in the mouth.	**a.** Don't let other people see your faults.
2. ____ Don't make waves.	**b.** Don't criticize a gift or an opportunity.
3. ____ Don't make a federal case out of it.	**c.** Don't talk about unrelated issues; get to the point.
4. ____ Don't stick your neck out.	**d.** Don't make plans before you have all the necessary information or items.
5. ____ Don't wash your dirty linen in public.	**e.** Don't bring up that topic.
6. ____ Don't count your chickens before they hatch.	**f.** Don't exaggerate a situation.
7. ____ Don't beat around the bush.	**g.** Don't interfere; don't cause problems.
8. ____ Don't go there.	**h.** Don't take unnecessary chances.

Freewriting means writing anything that comes to mind without worrying about grammar, spelling, and other writing conventions. It can help you become a more fluent writer.

7 **Freewriting** Write on the topic below for ten minutes without stopping. Give specific examples from your own experience to support your point of view.

> In your opinion, what is the best way to learn a foreign language: in a class, on your own (outside of class), or a combination of the two?

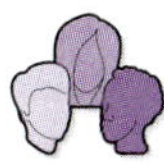

8 **Gathering Information** Find three people who speak a foreign language, and interview them about their language-learning experiences. Use the questionnaire on pages 5–6 and add your own questions.

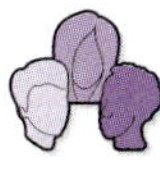

9 **Sharing Results** Share the results of your interviews with the class and discuss the following questions.

1. How many people thought that their ability in a foreign language was excellent?

   ____

2. How did most of the people learn their main foreign language? Did they learn it in a class or on their own?

   ____

   ____

3. How many people thought that a teacher was important for learning a language? How many people thought that they could have learned the language on their own?

   ____

   ____

4. What were the most interesting language-learning strategies that people had?

   ____

   ____

   ____

   ____

   ____

   ____

Part 2 Focusing on Words and Phrases

Describing Foreign Language Learning

1 Finding Meaning in Context Below are some words and expressions from "Want to Learn a Language? Don't Make It a Mount Everest." Find them in the passage. Notice their contexts—how they are used in a sentence—and try to guess their meanings. Then match the meanings on the right to the words and expressions on the left. Write the letters on the lines.

Words and Expressions	Meanings
____ **1.** criterion (Line 53)	**a.** a person who speaks more than one language
____ **2.** crucial (Line 42)	**b.** a course for learning something that you can use immediately, in a real situation
____ **3.** institute (Line 33)	**c.** the condition of being very good at something
____ **4.** polyglot (Line 10)	**d.** a way of learning a foreign language in which only the target language is spoken in class
____ **5.** native speakers (Lines 50–51)	**e.** people who speak a language as their first language
____ **6.** nonnative (Lines 55–56)	**f.** a quality or a value that you use to make a judgment
____ **7.** practical program (Line 19)	**g.** the language that you want to learn
____ **8.** proficiency (Line 32)	**h.** a person who does not speak a language as his or her first language
____ **9.** target language (Line 57)	**i.** extremely important
____ **10.** total immersion (Line 37)	**j.** a school or organization where learning takes place

2 Using Expressions

Study these expressions for discussing language learning. Notice the prepositions in each.

be good at
be successful at
be proficient in
succeed at
have success with
keep [someone] from VERB-ing
make [a lot of/a little] progress in

} + a subject or a skill

Examples

I'm good at language learning, but I'm not good at music.
Jason has made a lot of progress in Spanish this year.
A lack of free time keeps Rafael from learning Japanese.

Now complete the sentences. Use the correct prepositions.

1. Chris is proficient ____________ three languages: Spanish, English, and Japanese.
2. Jake has made a lot of progress ____________ French this year because he attended every class.
3. If you want to succeed ____________ speaking a foreign language, you must practice, practice, practice!
4. Anxiety can keep students ____________ becoming proficient ____________ a foreign language.
5. The class had a lot of success ____________ the lesson because they did their homework.

Paragraph Practice

3 Using New Words and Expressions

Use the new words and expressions from this section to complete the following activities:

1. Write a paragraph about someone you know who has or has not been successful at learning a foreign language. Use the expressions from activity 2.
2. Write a paragraph about one of the people that you interviewed for the language-learning questionaire on pages 5–6. Use the words and expressions on pages 12–13.
3. Rewrite your Freewriting from Part 1 using the words and expressions on pages 12-13.

▲ Reading foreign language newspapers

Part 3 Organizing and Developing Your Ideas

Essay Form and Function

Review Points

- In a paragraph, you develop and support one main idea.
- In an essay, you develop and support a thesis, which may contain more than one main idea.

New Points

- An essay usually has several paragraphs.
- The purpose of an essay is to express an idea or an opinion and support it.
- In an essay, you can analyze, explain, or describe someone or something; state an opinion and support it; show a relationship between two or more things; solve a problem; or a combination of all of these.

DISCOVERING THE ACADEMIC ESSAY

An academic essay usually contains the following parts:

- *An introductory paragraph,* which introduces the essay. The purpose of this paragraph is to make the reader interested in your topic.
- *A thesis or main idea statement,* which expresses the main idea of the essay. A thesis statement expresses your main ideas and can also suggest how you will develop your main ideas. The thesis statement usually appears in the introductory paragraph.

- *Body paragraphs,* each of which develops the main ideas that you express in your thesis statement. These paragraphs contain specific details, examples, and facts that illustrate your approach to the topic. They can also contain your interpretation or analysis of these details, examples, and facts. Transition words and phrases connect the ideas in these paragraphs (as well as the paragraphs themselves) to each other. These help the reader follow your ideas. In this course, you will be writing essays that have two or more body paragraphs.
- *A concluding paragraph,* which summarizes your main points and tells the reader that you have completed the essay. This paragraph is the last in the essay.

Note: Begin each paragraph in an essay by indenting the first line.

---

1 Studying the Parts of an Academic Essay Study the following diagram of an essay and label its parts.

Paragraph 1	Paragraph 4
__________________	__________________
Paragraph 2	Paragraph 5
__________________	__________________
Paragraph 3	Paragraph 6
__________________	__________________

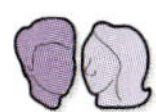

2 Analyzing an Academic Essay (Part 1) With a partner, read the following student essay. Then identify and label these parts:

- The introductory paragraph
- The thesis statement/main idea
- The body paragraphs
- Words and phrases that connect ideas
- The concluding paragraph

▲ Online language learning

Student Essay: The Benefits of Online Language Learning

A In today's global environment, knowing a foreign language is increasingly important. The ability to speak a foreign language with clarity and fluency is invaluable for business, education, and when working, living, or traveling in another country. Most foreign language teaching occurs in a classroom with an instructor, textbooks, and several students. In my opinion, however, one of the best ways to learn a foreign language is a self-study, online course. Online language learning is a good way to learn a second language because it's convenient, it's individualized, and it takes place in a low-stress environment.

B Classroom learning is not practical for many people due to time and cost constraints. In addition, taking time away from work or other responsibilities to attend language courses at an institution is difficult for many people. With a self-study, online course, students can take lessons at home or in the office whenever they want. All they need is a computer and an Internet connection. For example, a busy executive can take a language lesson during her lunch hour. A parent with small children can study online at night. In addition, because the student doesn't have to drive anywhere, online learning saves money.

C A benefit of online language learning is that it's individualized. Many online language courses have pre-tests that assess each student's level. Online language programs can also collect information about the student's learning style and need for studying the foreign language so that the material can be adapted to the student's actual situation. In a classroom, there are many students, each with different proficiency levels, different learning styles, and different needs for speaking a foreign language. Furthermore, because online material is not as static as it is in a textbook, it can be constantly updated and refreshed. This makes the learning experience more interesting and relevant for the student.

D Finally, with online learning, the learning takes place in a low-stress environment—a private setting with no one else around. This is very important because many studies have shown that stress and anxiety inhibit perception, performance, and retention of linguistic material. In a classroom with several other students, all at different levels and with different needs, students may feel inhibited and fearful of making a mistake. They may be afraid to try making new sounds or expressing their thoughts in the new language. In addition, an atmosphere of competition that exists in many classrooms can be deadly for some students. In fact, the fear of making mistakes or seeming foolish or childlike in front of others inhibits many people from succeeding in foreign language courses. Online learning solves all of these problems. Alone with a computer, a good online language course, and a microphone, many students can make tremendous progress without the fear of appearing foolish in front of others.

E The benefits of online self-study courses are that they are low-cost, people can do them at any time, and they can do them alone in the privacy of their own home or office. This last benefit is especially important in that many people feel less inhibited about acquiring and practicing language skills when they are alone. In addition, class size at many institutions limits the opportunities for foreign language students to get adequate individual attention. These are just a few of the reasons that an online course is a good way for many people to learn a foreign language.

3 Analyzing an Academic Essay

Answer these questions about the essay.

1. What is the main idea of the essay?

____

____

2. What is the writer's purpose in writing this essay? Check all of the choices that are correct.

_____ To analyze someone or something

_____ To explain someone or something

_____ To describe someone or something

_____ To state an opinion and support it

_____ To show a relationship between two or more things

_____ To solve a problem

_____ Other (explain) ______________________________

____

_____ A combination of the above

3. Are there connecting words and phrases within and between paragraphs? If so, what are they?

____

____

4. Is the essay easy to understand? Why or why not?

____

____

Writing Product

4 Writing About Language Learning Write an essay on the topic below. Express your opinion clearly. Also, remember to include:

- An introductory paragraph
- A thesis statement that expresses your main idea
- Two or more body paragraphs
- Connecting words and phrases
- A concluding paragraph

What do you think is the best way to learn a foreign language: in class, out of class, a combination of the two, or some other way? Write an essay to explain your opinion. Use the ideas that you've discussed and written about so far in this chapter. You may refer to the information you gathered from your interviews in Part 1.

TOEFL® IBT

Focus on Testing

Checking Your Responses

Activity 3 on page 17 asks you to identify parts of a student essay. Your written responses on the TOEFL® iBT test should have at least some parts mentioned in the activity:

- Introductory paragraph (with thesis statement)
- Body paragraphs

This list does not include a concluding paragraph, because the TOEFL® iBT rubric does not place any value on one. Your score will not be affected if there is no conclusion.

When you take the TOEFL® iBT test, you will have 30 minutes to write one response (the "independent" task) and 20 minutes to write the other (the "integrated" task). In such a short period of time, you are likely to need every minute to express the things you want to express. Still, you should leave about five minutes near the end of the time period to review and lightly edit your response. Check for all necessary parts. Are they there? Are they clear? If not, quickly try to make repairs.

Since all TOEFL® iBT test writing is done with a computer, you can rearrange sentences and paragraphs by copying and moving text. This helpful feature has to be used carefully. It can lead to so-called "cut-and-paste" errors. Check to make sure that:

- any pieces of text moved to another location fit well into place.
- after a piece of text has been removed, the text in its old location flows smoothly.

Word processing programs also allow you to fix spelling or word-choice errors. Again, be careful. Review any words or phrases you have retyped. If there are any extra letters—or missing letters—fix the problems.

Advice: Do most of your revising AFTER you have written the whole response. Most people get distracted and write inefficiently if they fix text errors as they are trying to express their ideas.

Practice: Choose one of the following prompts and write a response. Then revise it as much as you can in five minutes. Time limits for each prompt are given at the end of the prompt. With one or two other students, review each person's response and look for misplaced ideas, misspelled words, and other errors that could be easily fixed.

Prompts

1. Public universities in the United States allow students a great deal of academic and personal freedom. Students can choose many of their classes; live wherever they like (usually after their first year); and choose their own friends, activities, and schedules. Do think this freedom is good or bad for students? Support your point of view with specific examples, details, or reasons. *(25 minutes to plan and write a response; 5 minutes to revise)*

2. The reading about continental climates (like the climate of the Great Plains states in the U.S.) and the lecture about maritime climates (like those of England or the Pacific coast of the U.S. and Canada) mention several factors that influence climate. Explain these factors. Support your explanations with specific examples, details, and reasons. *(15 minutes to plan and write a response; 5 minutes to revise)*

   Note: Since you do not have either the reading or the lecture mentioned in this prompt, you may want to research maritime and continental climates for about 45 minutes in a library or on the Internet. If you do not research these topics, don't worry. You can make up your own "facts" for the purposes of this exercise.

3. Using information from the reading and the lecture, explain how certain bacteria can be both helpful and harmful to humans. Support your explanation with specific examples, details, or reasons. *(15 minutes to plan and write a response; 5 minutes to revise)*

   Note: Since you do not have either the reading or the lecture mentioned in this prompt, you may want to research the topic of helpful and harmful bacteria for about 45 minutes in a library or on the Internet. If you do not research this topic, don't worry. You can make up your own "facts" for the purposes of this exercise.

Part 4 Evaluating Your Writing

Use the following holistic rubric to score your writing. A holistic rubric evaluates the "whole" of your paragraph, not the separate "pieces." Read the rubric with your class, and then give your writing a score. A classmate and a teacher will score your writing also. If you want to revise and improve your paragraph, you can do it now or you can wait and do it after Chapter 3.

Rubric for Writing about Learning a New Language

Score	Description
3 **Excellent**	■ **Content:** Writing presents clear opinion and supports opinion with reasons, examples, and/or facts to convince the reader. ■ **Form:** Ideas are presented in an essay which includes an introduction, main idea, body paragraphs, and a conclusion. ■ **Vocabulary and Sentence Structure:** Writing is correct; mistakes don't interfere with writer's meaning.
2 **Adequate**	■ **Content:** Writing presents an opinion; reasons, examples, and/or facts can be brief and reader may not be convinced. ■ **Form:** Some essay parts may be missing. ■ **Vocabulary and Sentence Structure:** Writing is mostly correct; there are a few mistakes.
1 **Developing**	■ **Content:** Writing does not present opinion clearly or does not support opinion with sufficient reasons, examples, and/or facts. ■ **Form:** Ideas do not follow essay format and are confusing. ■ **Vocabulary and Sentence Structure:** There are too many mistakes to understand and/or follow the ideas.

Self-Assessment Log

In this chapter, you worked through the following activities. How much did they help you become a better writer? Check *A lot*, *A little*, or *Not at all*.

	A lot	**A little**	**Not at all**
I discussed photos of people speaking a second language.	❏	❏	❏
I read about learning a second language.	❏	❏	❏
I recognized cultural references.	❏	❏	❏
I interviewed people about their language-learning experiences.	❏	❏	❏
I learned to use vocabulary for writing about language learning.	❏	❏	❏
I discovered essay form and function.	❏	❏	❏
I wrote and evaluated my essay.	❏	❏	❏
(Add something) ________________________________	❏	❏	❏

____

Chapter 2

Danger and Daring

In This Chapter

Genre Focus: Information

Writing Product

In this chapter, you'll write about an explorer.

Writing Process

- Discuss photos of explorers.
- Read about women mountain climbers.
- Make predictions.
- Gather information about a person who has done. something daring and dangerous.
- Learn and use vocabulary for describing explorers.
- Write thesis statements.
- Provide supporting information.

"Exploration is really the essence of the human spirit."

—Frank Borman
American astronaut (1928–)

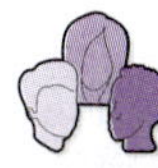

Connecting to the Topic

1. Why do people do daring and dangerous things?
2. Have you ever done anything daring or dangerous?
3. Do you know of someone who has done something daring or dangerous?

Part 1 Preparing to Write

Getting Started

1 Discussing Explorers Since the beginning of human history, people have left familiar places to explore different parts of the world. What motivates these explorers? Look at the following photos of some explorers. Scan the information about them. Complete the chart on page 25, and then answer the questions that follow.

▲ Matthew Henson (American) was the co-discoverer of the North Pole with Robert Peary in 1909.

▲ Sydney Possuelo (Brazilian) is an Amazonian rainforest explorer. He received the Patron's Medal of the Royal Geographical Society in 2004.

▲ Chiaki Mukai (Japanese) was the first Japanese woman to fly in space and was part of a NASA mission in 1985.

▲ Arlene Blum (American) was the leader of the first group of American climbers to reach the the top of Annapurna in 1972.

Who Was This Explorer?	Where Was He or She From?	What Did He or She Do?	When Did He or She Do It?
		First Japanese woman to fly in space	
	China		
Sydney Possuelo			
			1972

1. Which of these explorers seems the most interesting? Why?

____

____

2. Which explorers are you familiar with? Which did you learn about for the first time?

____

____

3. Look at the information on two of the explorers. What dangers do you think they faced? What do you think motivated them to travel to the unfamiliar places?

____

____

4. Have you ever thought of exploring something? Why or why not?

____

____

2 Brainstorming Think of other types of explorers (for example, people who discovered new places or developed new ideas). They can be from any country and from any time period. Write their names and major achievements in the chart below.

Names	Major Achievements

In 1978, Arlene Blum led a group to the top of Annapurna I (26,603 feet/8108.5 meters), a mountain in Nepal. Not only was this the first group of Americans to reach the top, but it was the first all-woman expedition to Annapurna I. When Arlene Blum returned, she wrote a book about her experiences. The following selection is from her book, *Annapurna: A Woman's Place.* In the selection you will read, Blum gives the history of women and mountain climbing.

3 Preparing to Read

Before you read, answer the following questions.

1. Annapurna is a large mountain range in the Himalaya Mountains. What do you know about the Himalayan region? What words and images come to mind when you think about it?

   ____

   ____

2. Are there particular personality characteristics a mountain climber must have? What are they?

   ____

   ____

3. Have you ever done any mountain climbing or gone hiking in the mountains? If so, where? Did you enjoy it? Why or why not?

   ____

   ____

4. What kind of physical condition is helpful for a mountain climber to be in? Why is being in good physical condition important?

   ____

   ____

Annapurna: A Woman's Place

A It is clear that women mountain climbers have felt the urge to explore remote regions and ascend high peaks for many years. *On Top of the World: Five Women Explorers in Tibet* describes five of the many women who explored the high Himalayas between 1850 and 1920. One of them, Isabella Byrd, had been sickly for most of her life in England, but she experienced a dramatic change as she traveled at high elevations in Kashmir. Unlike her experiences in England, as a pioneer and traveler she laughed at fatigue, she was unafraid of danger, and she didn't worry about her next meal.

B Another woman explorer of her time was Alexandra David-Neel from France. Her journeys across the high Tibetan plateau from 1911 to 1944 have been characterized as the most remarkable ever made by any explorer, man or woman, in Tibet. At the age of 55 she disguised herself as a Tibetan beggar woman and walked two thousand miles across numerous high snowy passes to reach the forbidden city of Lhasa.

C Fanny Bullock Workman and her husband, Dr. W. H. Workman, of Massachusetts, traveled and explored in the Himalayas between 1890 and 1915. They wrote six books about their adventures. Fanny, an ardent suffragette, was once photographed on a high pass in the Himalayas carrying a newspaper bearing the headline "Votes for Women."

D Another early woman climber and a rival of Mrs. Workman was Annie S. Peck, a New England professor. She began her climbing career with an ascent of the Matterhorn when she was 45. In 1908, at the age of 58, she made the first ascent of Huascaran, the highest mountain in Peru. At 21,837 feet, she claimed it was the altitude record for any American. Peck described herself as a "firm believer in the equality of the sexes . . . [A]ny great achievement in any line of endeavor would be an advantage to my sex." (Annie S. Peck, *High Mountain Climbing in Peru and Bolivia*, 1912)

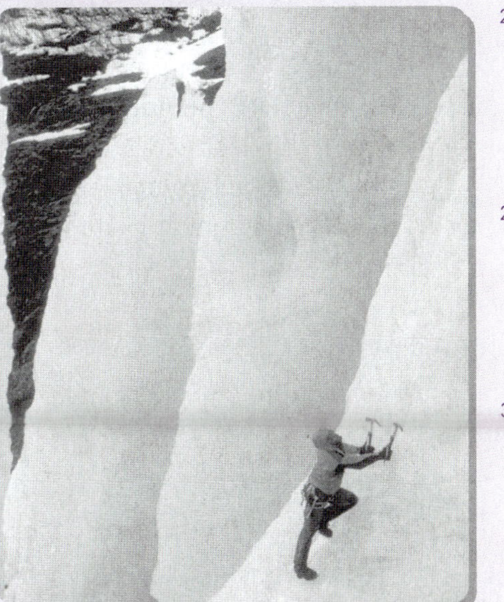

▲ Climbing Annapurna

E In the years since World War II, women have made numerous significant climbs in the Andes and the Himalayas. One of the most remarkable of them was the late French climber Claude Kogan. British women have also been successful climbers. From the 1950s onward, they have carried out many small, well-organized expeditions to previously unexplored regions of the Himalayas and written about them in an understated, characteristically British fashion. In addition to the British and other small expeditions, women climbers throughout the world have made significant contributions to climbing in the last 100 years. However, until quite recently, women have been notably absent on the world's highest mountains. There are 14 mountains in the world that soar above 8,000 meters (26,200 feet)—all located in the Himalayas. For many years, mountaineers have wanted to figure out a way to reach their summits. Attempts to climb them began in the nineteenth century; in the first half of the twentieth century, hundreds of men participated in dozens of expeditions to these peaks. But even after Fanny Workman's example, only a handful of women participated in such climbs. Elizabeth Knowlton was a member of the joint German-American climb to Nanga Parbat in 1932. In 1934 Hettie Dyhrenfurth took part in an expedition that explored and mapped the Baltoro Glacier region of the Karakoram Himalaya; she reached the top of Queen Mary Peak (24,370 feet), which gave her the world altitude record for women for which Annie Peck and Fanny Workman had competed.

F It was not until 1950 that an 8,000-meter peak was climbed by anyone. The legendary ascent of Annapurna I by Maurice Herzog's French team was closely followed by successes on all 8,000-meter giants over the next 14 years—and all by men. During this period the only attempt on an 8,000-meter peak by a woman's team was the ill-fated 1959 International Woman's Expedition to Cho Oyu in Nepal. Tragically, four climbers, including the leader, Claude Kogan, died in this attempt. By 1972, when the idea for our all-woman expedition to Annapurna was originally conceived, no women from any country had yet reached the summit of an 8,000-meter peak.

—Arlene Blum, *Annapurna: A Woman's Place.*

4 Understanding the Reading Summarize the information from the reading selection by filling in the following graphic organizer. Skim the reading selection for details about the women explorers that Blum describes. Note their home countries, the years in which they traveled, and their achievements.

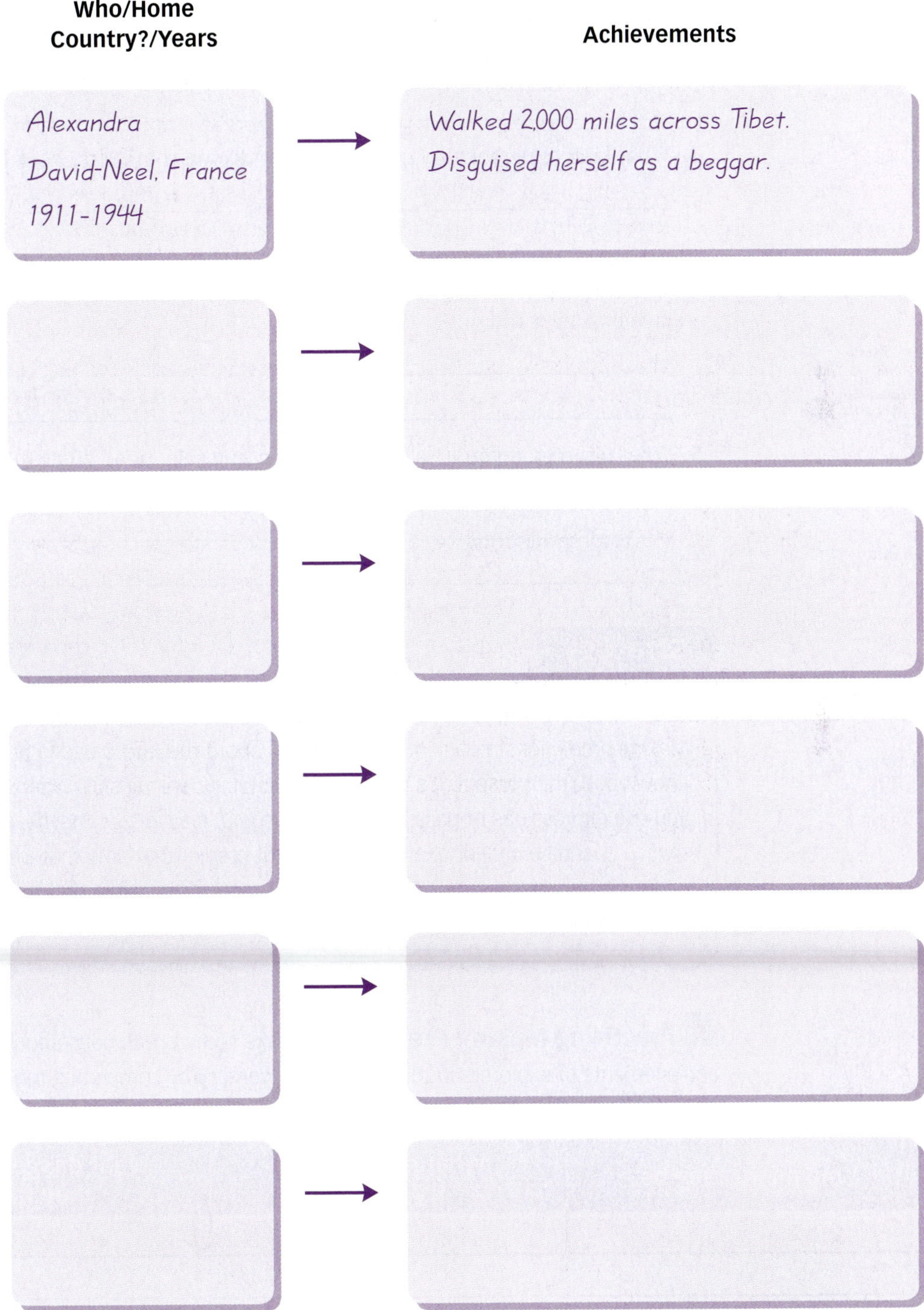

Who/Home Country?/Years
Achievements
Alexandra David-Neel, France 1911-1944
Walked 2,000 miles across Tibet. Disguised herself as a beggar.

5 In small groups, answer the following questions.

1. Why was Alexandra David-Neel's journey through Tibet remarkable?

   ____

   ____

2. Fanny Bullock Workman was a suffragette. What is a suffragette?

   ____

   ____

3. What kind of personality characteristics do you think Mrs. Peck had?

   ____

   ____

4. What are some obstacles women climbers have faced? Do you think they still face obstacles today?

   ____

   ____

5. What interested you most about this reading selection? What would you like to know more about?

   ____

   ____

Strategy

Thinking Critically: *Making Predictions*

Making predictions means making guesses about the future based on what you know about the present. It's an important critical thinking skill. When you predict, you use expressions of possibility such as *could, may, might, maybe, It's possible that . . .* , and so on. For example, you might predict that now that Chiaki Mukai and other Japanese women have flown in space, it's possible that many more Japanese women will become astronauts.

6 **Practicing Making Predictions** Make some predictions about possible achievements of explorers in the twenty-first century by completing the following chart. What will they do?

Who might they be?	What might they try to do?	What dangers might they face?

7 Freewriting

Write for 15 minutes about the topic below.

> Think about the explorers you've read about and discussed in this section. What do these people have in common? What motivated them to do what they did? Money? Fame? Ambition? National loyalty? A sense of adventure? Personal pride?

8 Gathering Information

Find out more about an explorer from this section or about someone else who interests you: an explorer, an athlete, a scientist, an astronaut, etc. Choose anyone who has accomplished something daring or dangerous, or who has accomplished something that no one has ever done before. As you read about the person, take notes, and try to find answers to as many of the following questions as possible.

1. What was the person's background (nationality, time, and culture in which he or she lived, and so on)?
2. How would you describe his or her personality?
3. How and why did this person become an explorer (or other profession)?
4. What particular types of danger did this person face?
5. How did he or she overcome the danger?
6. What were his or her achievements?

9 Sharing Results

Give a presentation on the person you researched. Try to find a picture of the person to show to the class. Prepare for your presentation completing the following list:

1. Name: ____________________
2. Nationality: ____________________
   ____
3. Main achievement(s): ____________________
   ____
   ____
4. Dates of main achievement(s): ____________________
   ____
5. Motivation for becoming an explorer (or other profession): ____________________
   ____
   ____

(continued on the next page)

6. Challenges the person faced: ______________________________

____

____

7. How the person overcame the challenges: ______________________________

____

____

8. The person's characteristics: ______________________________

____

____

9. Other interesting or relevant information: ______________________________

____

____

10. Your personal reaction to or opinion of this person: ______________________________

____

____

Part 2 Focusing on Words and Phrases

Describing Explorers

1 Finding Meaning in Context Below are some words and expressions from "Annapurna: A Woman's Place" on page 27. Find them in the passage. Notice their contexts—how they are used in a sentence—and try to guess their meanings. Then match the meanings on the right to the words and expressions on the left. Write the letters on the lines.

Words and Expressions	Meanings
c 1. ardent (Line 17)	**a.** person who is competing against another
e 2. ascent (Line 27)	**b.** far away from civilization
i 3. endeavor *(n.)* (Line 34)	**c.** passionate; enthusiastic
h 4. felt the urge (Line 1)	**d.** obviously not present
g 5. summit (Line 50)	**e.** climb
j 6. legendary (Line 61)	**f.** someone who is the first to explore a new place
d 7. notably absent (Line 47)	**g.** the top of a mountain

___f___ **8.** pioneer (Line 7)	**h.** had a very strong desire
___b___ **9.** remote (Line 2)	**i.** effort; an attempt
___a___ **10.** rival (Line 21)	**j.** famous

EXPRESSIONS TO DESCRIBE PERSONALITIES AND ACHIEVEMENTS OF EXPLORERS

The following list of expressions from "Annapurna: A Woman's Place" on page 27 can be used to discuss the personalities and achievements of explorers. Notice and try to memorize the prepositions in each.

Personalities

be unafraid of (danger)
laugh at (fatigue)
not worry about (her next meal)
figure out a way to

Achievements

travel at (high elevations)
carry out (expeditions)
make significant contributions to
participate in (expeditions)
take part in (expeditions)
reach the summit of

Examples

Bachendri Pal was the first Indian woman to reach the summit of Mount Everest.
An astronaut must be unafraid of danger.
Sydney Possuelo has made significant contributions to our knowledge of the Amazon.

2 **Using Expressions** Complete the sentences with the correct prepositions. Try to do this without looking at the expressions above.

1. Mark took part ___in___ several expeditions to the summits of mountains in the Himalayan region.
2. A scientist who tries to figure ___out___ a way ___to___ cure cancer is also a kind of explorer.
3. Many of the early female explorers didn't worry ___about___ hunger or fatigue.
4. Chris laughs ___at___ danger; she has no fear.
5. Jake participated ___in___ a 500-mile hike in Northern Australia last fall.
6. Arlene Blum has carried ___out___ many mountaineering expeditions.

Paragraph Practice

3 Using New Words and Expressions Use the new words and expressions learned in this section to complete the following activities:

1. Choose one of the explorers you've read about or researched in this chapter and write about him or her using words and expressions from this section. Use your knowledge of the explorers, the photos in Part 1, and your imagination to make your writing interesting.
2. Imagine that you are on a government committee hiring a person to travel into space to make some important discoveries. In a paragraph, describe the characteristics this person should have. Use the words and expressions from this section.
3. Rewrite your freewriting from Activity 7 on page 11 using the words and expressions on pages 32–33.

Part 3 Organizing And Developing Your Ideas

The Thesis Statement: Topic and Approach

Review Points

- An essay is composed of three or more paragraphs and communicates an attitude or opinion about an issue.
- The thesis statement tells the reader the main idea of the essay.
- The reader should be able to predict what the essay is about by reading the thesis statement.
- The thesis statement usually appears in the introductory paragraph.

New Points

- The thesis statement usually contains two parts: the topic and the approach to the topic.
- The topic presents the general subject of the essay.
- The approach presents the writer's attitude or opinion about the topic and indicates how the writer will develop the essay.

STUDYING AN EXAMPLE OF A THESIS STATEMENT

Read the following thesis statement:

> Sydney Possuelo is a great explorer because he has not only made significant contributions to our knowledge of the Amazon but has also worked to defend the rights of the indigenous people of Brazil.

In this thesis statement, the topic is Sydney Possuelo. The writer's approach is to show why Possuelo is a great explorer. From this thesis statement, the reader can predict that the writer will explain that Possuelo has increased our knowledge of the Amazon while also defending the rights of the indigenous (native) people who live in that region.

---

1 Analyzing Thesis Statements

For the thesis statements that follow, underline the topic and put a dashed line under the approach.

1. Many explorers have the urge to explore due to their own curiosity and a desire to make a contribution to the world.
2. The adventures of medieval travelers such as Marco Polo and Ibn Battuta led to cross-cultural exchange and expanded international trade.
3. Alexander the Great was one of the ancient world's greatest explorers because he solved many mysteries about the earth's geography and weather.

2 Making Predictions from Thesis Statements

Look at the thesis statements in Activity 1. Predict how each writer will develop an essay based on the information in the thesis statement.

Thesis Statement 1: *The writer will explain how curiosity and the desire to make a contribution motivate many explorers.*

Thesis Statement 2: ______________________________

Thesis Statement 3: ______________________________

Supporting Ideas

New Points

- The approach may include two or more supporting ideas about the topic.
- The writer will generally develop these ideas in separate paragraphs.
- Each supporting idea should have the same degree of generality or specificity.
- Each supporting idea should have the same degree of importance in relation to the topic.
- Each supporting idea should be distinct.

ANALYZING SUPPORTING IDEAS

In the thesis statement about Sydney Possuelo on page 35, the supporting ideas are (1) he has made significant contributions to our knowledge of the Amazon, and (2) he has worked to defend the rights of the indigenous people of Brazil.

Note the following:

- Making *contributions* and *defending rights* are equally general topics; one isn't more specific than the other.
- Both have the same degree of importance in relation to why Possuelo is a great explorer.
- They don't overlap; *making contributions* is different from *defending indigenous people's rights*. They can each be discussed in their own parts of the essay.

3 Revising Thesis Statements The following three thesis statements need rewriting. Working with a partner, decide what's wrong and rewrite each one according to the guidelines above.

1. Space exploration and undersea exploration have two things in common: both are motivated by the thirst for knowledge and the desire to learn more about the world.
   What's wrong? same meaning
2. Yuri Gagarin's single orbit of the earth on April 12, 1961, was newsworthy because the Russian cosmonaut was the first man to travel in space and the name of his spaceship was Vostok.
   What's wrong? too specific

3. Although Alan Shepard and Yuri Gagarin represented different countries, their early flights in space took them both to altitudes of over a hundred miles and increased our knowledge of humans' ability to live in space.
What's wrong?

4 Identifying Topic and Supporting Ideas Read each of the following thesis statements. Underline the topic and put a dashed line under the supporting ideas. If the thesis statement is good, circle *good.* If it is not good, circle *needs work* and rewrite it according to what you learned in this section.

1. The Brazilian explorer Sydney Possuelo risked his life when he tried to protect the Korubo Indians of the Amazon.
   good *needs work*
   Rewrite:

2. From earliest times, humans have been driven by a desire to know the unknown and to find food.
   good *needs work*
   Rewrite:

3. Ferdinand Magellan and Christopher Columbus, two fifteenth-century sailors, were similar because they believed they could find a westward passage to India and because they received no support for their beliefs.
   good *needs work*
   Rewrite:

4. Great strides in space exploration were made in 1984, when two American astronauts floated free in space: They gathered some important information about humans' ability to live in space and returned to the spacecraft on their own.
   good *needs work*
   Rewrite:

5. Amelia Earhart was the first woman to fly a plane across the Atlantic.
   good *needs work*
   Rewrite:

5 **Writing Thesis Statements** The following are sets of notes on topics related to explorers and exploring. Read the notes and then write a good thesis statement for each set below.

Set 1

Jacques Cousteau

- *Born in France in 1910*
- *Undersea explorer*
- *Helped invent the aqualung, which enables people to breathe underwater*
- *Wrote The Silent World*
- *Perfected watertight movie cameras*
- *Salvaged cargo from many sunken ships underwater*
- *Made many films*
- *Invented the bathyscaphe, which enables observation two miles below the surface of the water*

Set 2

Dangers in Space

- *People in space are totally dependent on their vehicle.*
- *Meteors can tear holes in spaceships.*
- *Cosmic rays could be a threat.*
- *If people travel far from Earth, certain kinds of radiation could be harmful.*
- *Ultraviolet rays could cause burns.*

Cousteau

___

___

___

Dangers in Space

___

___

___

TOEFL® IBT

Focus on Testing

Writing Thesis Statements

You just learned about writing a good thesis statement. This is especially challenging on the TOEFL® iBT test, which gives you very little time to plan, write, and review your responses. Time that you would ordinarily spend in carefully deciding on a thesis statement is simply not available under TOEFL® iBT conditions. This means that you have to compose a strong thesis statement quickly and without a lot of thought.

The best way to find the basis for a thesis statement is to look carefully at the prompt. It contains ideas, and even phrases, that can guide you to a relevant and meaningful thesis statement.

Practice Read the following sample prompts. Identify and underline parts of each prompt that could be paraphrased to make a good thesis statement. Then write a thesis statement for a response. The first two are done for you as examples.

1. **Prompt:** Because accidents have been increasing, the university is considering closing many roads to cars. Only foot traffic and bicyclists would be allowed on these roads. Do you think this is a good idea or not?

   Sample thesis statement: Keeping cars off many university roads would definitely reduce the number of accidents on campus.

2. **Prompt:** Using information from both the reading and the lecture, explain the goals of the U.S. Social Security system.

   Sample thesis statement: Both the reading and the lecture point out that the Social Security system in the U.S. aims to provide basic financial support for retired persons and for disabled workers.

   Note: In this situation, certain phrases (e.g., *Social Security system*) from the prompt should be directly borrowed because there is no convenient way to paraphrase them.

3. **Prompt:** How does the lecture cast doubt on the reading's claims about the dangers of traveling by airplane?

   Sample thesis statement:

   ____

   ____

   ____

   Note: The phrase *cast doubt on something* means "cause you to think something is not true." It is very common in TOEFL® iBT prompts, so you should get used to seeing and using it.

4. **Prompt:** Most universities offer students free access to the Internet. Would you prefer to get most of your news through the Internet or through a more traditional source, such as television or newspapers? Support your choice with specific reasons.

   Sample thesis statement:

   ____

   ____

   ____

5. Prompt: Describe the influence that a teacher, counselor, or other school official has had on your academic life. Support your claim that this person has been influential with specific examples or details.

   Sample thesis statement:

   ____

   ____

   ____

Writing Product

6 Writing about Explorers

Write an essay about the following topic:

> Choose one of the explorers presented in this chapter or someone else who has "explored" in other ways, and write an essay about him or her. You might consider one of the following people:
>
> - Isaac Newton
> - Marie Curie
> - Mohandas Gandhi
> - Malcolm X
> - Ibn Battuta
> - Wangari Maathai

Do library or Internet research to get information about the explorer you've chosen. If you do Internet research, try putting the person's name into a search engine such as Google™ (google.com). Put quotes around the person's name. This way, you get fewer results.

In writing your essay, use the ideas, words, and expressions discussed in this chapter. Remember to:

- help the reader "get to know" the explorer you've chosen.
- describe the explorer and his or her accomplishment(s), motivation, challenges, and other facts.
- make sure your thesis statement contains two parts—the topic and the approach to the topic.

▲ Underwater explorer

Part 4 Evaluating Your Writing

Use the following rubric to score your writing. Read the rubric with your class, then give your writing a score. A classmate and a teacher will score your writing also and explain reasons for their scores. If you want to revise and improve your essay, you can do it now or you can wait and do it after Chapter 3.

Rubric for Writing About an Explorer

Score	Description
3 **Excellent**	▪ **Content:** Writing presents an explorer and develops a complete characterization through description, accomplishment(s), motivations, challenges, and/or facts to help the reader get to know the person. ▪ **Organization:** Ideas are organized to support and explain main idea through an introduction, a main idea, body paragraphs, and a conclusion; ideas follow a logical sequence and are easy to follow. ▪ **Vocabulary and Sentence Structure:** Vocabulary is specific and descriptive; sentence types are varied. ▪ **Grammar:** Subjects and verbs agree; common grammar problems (pronouns, articles, and plurals) are minimal so that meaning is clear. ▪ **Spelling and Mechanics:** Most words are spelled correctly and punctuation is correct.
2 **Adequate**	▪ **Content:** Writing presents an explorer and develops a description through accomplishment(s), motivations, challenges, and/or facts. ▪ **Organization:** Ideas are organized and there is a clear beginning, middle and end; main idea is clear; some parts may be undeveloped. ▪ **Vocabulary and Sentence Structure:** Vocabulary is descriptive; sentences are mostly the same type. ▪ **Grammar:** Subjects and verbs mostly agree; common grammar problems (pronouns, articles, and plurals) are distracting. ▪ **Spelling and Mechanics:** Some distracting spelling and/or punctuation mistakes are included.

1 **Developing**	▪ **Content:** Writing does not present an explorer clearly or does not develop characterization with sufficient details. ▪ **Organization:** Ideas do not follow essay format and are confusing or too brief. ▪ **Vocabulary and Sentence Structure:** Vocabulary is limited and/or there are too many mistakes to understand and/or follow the ideas; sentences have mistakes. ▪ **Grammar:** Many common grammar problems (pronouns, articles, and plurals) appear that are confusing to the reader. ▪ **Spelling and Mechanics:** Many distracting spelling and/or punctuation mistakes are made.

Self-Assessment Log

In this chapter, you worked through the following activities. How much did each of them help you become a better writer? Check *A lot*, *A little*, or *Not at all*.

	A lot	A little	Not at all
I read about mountain climbers.	❑	❑	❑
I discussed explorers with my classmates.	❑	❑	❑
I gathered information about a person who has done something daring and dangerous.	❑	❑	❑
I studied words for describing explorers.	❑	❑	❑
I wrote thesis statements.	❑	❑	❑
I provided supporting information.	❑	❑	❑
I evaluated my essay.	❑	❑	❑
(Add something) ________________________________ ________________________________	❑	❑	❑

Chapter 3

Gender and Relationships

In This Chapter

Genre Focus: Descriptive

Writing Product

In this chapter, you'll write about communication style differences between men and women.

Writing Process

- Discuss photos of women and men communicating.
- Read about gender differences in communication.
- Recognize supporting information from experts.
- Collect examples of the differences between male. and female communication styles.
- Learn and use vocabulary for discussing differences.
- Develop paragraphs by answering readers' questions.

"The biggest mistake is believing there is one right way to listen, to talk, to have a conversation—or a relationship."

—Deborah Tannen
American sociolinguistics professor (1951–)

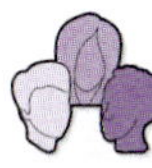

Connecting to the Topic

1. When is it easy to talk to a person of the opposite sex?
2. When is it difficult to talk to a person of the opposite sex?
3. What kinds of communication problems do men and women sometimes have?

Part 1 Preparing to Write

Getting Started

1 Discussing Gender Communication Styles Look at the following photos and read the captions. Then answer the questions that follow.

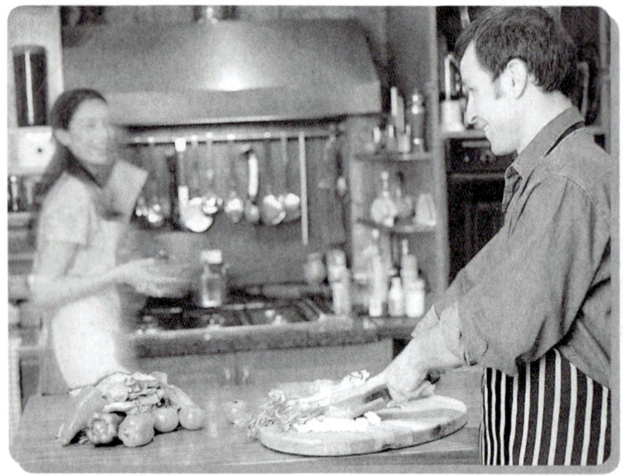

▲ MAN: Will you please go to the store for some eggs?

▲ WOMAN: I really need a few things from the store, but I'm so tired.

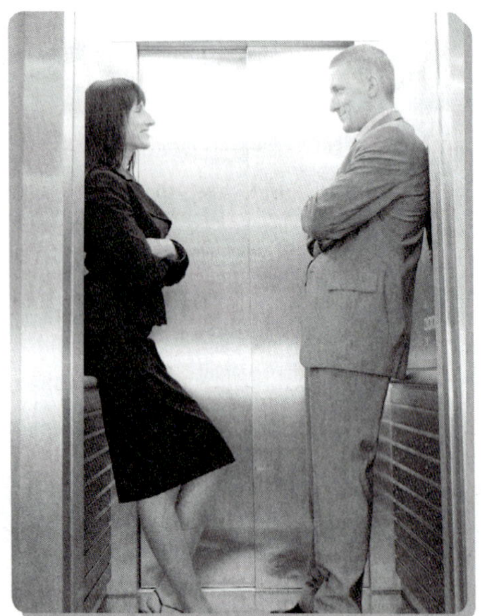

▲ MAN: It's a nice day.

▲ WOMAN: It's a nice day, isn't it?

1. Are the men and women in the pairs of photos saying the same thing?

____

____

2. What is the difference between what the man in each photo is saying and what the woman in each photo is saying?

____

____

3. What is the reason for the difference, in your opinion?

____

____

2 **Brainstorming** Form small groups, including both male and female classmates in each. Discuss communication difficulties that each of you sometimes has with the opposite sex. Try to think of the reasons for these difficulties. Choose one student to take notes on the group's ideas. When you have finished, have one student report on the results of your brainstorming session. As a class, compare your results. Did you find the same difficulties appear over and over again? Do you agree or disagree on the reasons for the difficulties? What affect does age or culture have on your ideas about gender communication?

3 **Preparing to Read** The reading selection on page 48 is about the differences between men and women's communication styles in English. Before you read, answer the following questions.

1. Who do you think has a more direct style of communication in your first language, men or women?

____

2. Who do you think is more likely to do each of the following, men or women?

   a. Want to talk about feelings _______________

   b. Use language to try to become closer to others _______________

   c. Interrupt _______________

   d. Insult others or not care about being insulted by others

   ____

3. When you read discussion-board postings or chat on the Internet, can you usually tell if the person writing is a man or woman? Why or why not?

____

____

Gender Differences in Communication

A All of us have different styles of communicating with other people. Our style depends on a lot of things: where we're from, how and where we were raised, our educational background, and our age. It also can depend on our gender. Generally speaking, men and women talk differently, although there are varying degrees of masculine and feminine speech characteristics in each of us. But women do speak in very particular ways that are associated with gender.

B Some researchers describe the styles that men and women use to communicate as "debate vs. relate," "report vs. rapport," or "competitive vs. cooperative" (with the first term in each pair describing men). In other words, men often seek direct solutions to problems and useful advice, whereas women tend to try to establish intimacy by discussing problems and showing concern and empathy.

C In her book *Women, Men and Language* (New York: Longman Inc., 1986), Jennifer Coates studied men-only and women-only discussion groups. She found that when women talk to each other, they reveal a lot about their private lives. They also stick to one topic for a long time, let all speakers finish their sentences, and try to have everyone participate. Men, on the other hand, rarely talk about their personal relationships and feelings, but "compete to prove themselves better informed about current affairs, travel, and sports." They change topics often and try to dominate the conversation.

D Dr. Lillian Glass's book *He Says, She Says: Closing the Communication Gap Between the Sexes* (The Putnam Berkeley Group) presents her findings on the many differences in the way men and women communicate, both verbally and nonverbally. For example, she found among other things that men speak more loudly than women do, that they interrupt more often than women do, and that they use fewer intensifiers ("really," "much," "quite") than women. She also found that while men make more declarative statements, women make statements sound like questions by using tags and question intonation ("It's a nice day, isn't it?") at the end of statements.

E What about online communication? Can one determine another person's gender just by reading their written words? Susan Herring thinks so. In a 1994 talk at a panel called "Making the Net *Work*," she said that men and women have recognizably different styles on the Internet. Her research showed that on Internet discussion boards, men tended to be more assertive than women. Women, in contrast, tended to hedge (be unsure), apologize, and ask questions. Men also appeared to enjoy, or at least tolerate, "flaming" (insulting others online), whereas women disliked and avoided it.

▲ Chatting on the Internet

F In other research, Gladys We, in her graduate research paper "Cross-Gender Communication in Cyberspace," discusses the results of a survey that she sent to both men and women about the importance of gender online. Author We discovered that most people felt that gender was relatively unimportant when they communicated online. Furthermore, We thinks that online communication leads to all the misunderstandings and confusions of face-to-face communication between men and women; however, she feels that it is potentially liberating because people can be anonymous.

–Adapted from: Rose Ker, "Gender Differences in Communication," and Gladys We, "Cross-Gender Communication in Cyberspace."

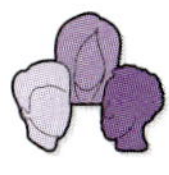

4 Understanding the Reading In small groups, answer the following questions.

1. According to the reading passage, what are some differences in face-to-face communication styles between men and women?

2. According to the passage, what are some differences in the online communication styles of men and women?

3. Give an example from your own experience of each of these communication style differences: (a) "debate vs. relate," (b) "report vs. rapport," and (c) "competitive vs. cooperative."

4. What does Gladys We mean when she says that online communication "is potentially liberating"? Do you agree?

Strategy

Thinking Critically: *Recognizing Supporting Information from Experts*

Experts are people with special qualifications in a particular field. Writers often give examples, descriptions, and explanations from experts to support their main ideas. This helps the reader to understand the author's ideas, and it also makes them seem more valid (true), because other people have done research to prove them.

5 Finding Supporting Information Who are the experts that the author of "Gender Differences in Communication" uses to support the idea that men and women have different communication styles? Complete the following chart with their names, their qualifications, and an example of their findings.

Name	Qualifications	Findings
Jennifer Coates		
	Wrote *He Says, She Says: Closing the Communication Gap Between the Sexes*	.
		Men are more assertive than women are on discussion boards.
Gladys We		

6 Freewriting Write on the topic below for 15 minutes without stopping.

> Think of problems that you have had communicating with the opposite sex. Describe one or more situations in which you have misunderstood or been misunderstood by a member of the opposite sex.

7 Gathering Information Collect examples of the differences between male and female communication styles. Look for examples by watching movies, plays, or TV shows that feature male-female relationships; or by watching people in public places such as school, work, or a restaurant. Look for the differences described in the article "Gender Differences in Communication" as well as for others, such as interrupting, body language, word choice, conversation topic choice, boasting/bragging, or swearing. Take notes on the differences that you notice.

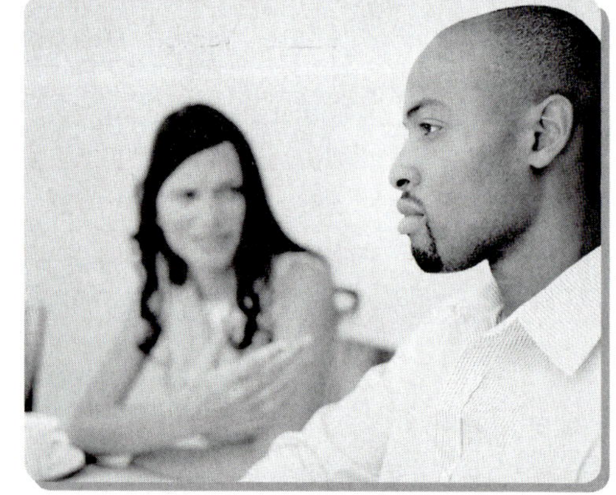

▲ An example of different communication styles

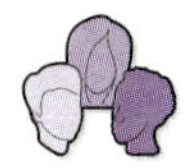

8 Sharing Results In small groups, report on the examples of male and female communication style differences that you observed in your research. If possible, illustrate the differences you found by reenacting a scene from a movie, TV show, or play that you saw.

Part 2 Focusing on Words and Phrases

Discussing Communication Differences

1 Finding Meaning in Context Here are some words and expressions from "Gender Differences in Communication" on pages 48–49. Find them in the passage. Notice their contexts—how they are used in a sentence—and try to guess their meanings. Then match the meanings on the right to the words and expressions on the left. Write the letters on the lines.

	Words and Expressions	Meanings
m	**1.** anonymous (Line 49)	**a.** different
k	**2.** assertive (Line 38)	**b.** ways of speaking
c	**3.** associated with (Line 7)	**c.** related to or caused by
i	**4.** dominate (Line 22)	**d.** connect with; interact with another person
g	**5.** empathy (Line 13)	**e.** having an understanding with another person; mutual understanding
j	**6.** findings (Line 25)	**f.** closeness
f	**7.** intimacy (Line 12)	**g.** feeling what another person feels
l	**8.** liberating (Line 49)	**h.** stay with
e	**9.** rapport (Line 9)	**i.** have control or power over
d	**10.** relate (Line 9)	**j.** results of research
b	**11.** speech characteristics (Line 6)	**k.** speaking with confidence
h	**12.** stick to (Line 17)	**l.** freeing
a	**13.** varying (Line 5)	**m.** unknown; not named

SHOWING SIMILARITIES AND DIFFERENCES

When you compare and contrast, you show the similarities or differences between two or more things. The passage that you read on pages 48–49 contains certain words and expressions that show a contrast between the communication styles of men and women. For example: "While men make more declarative statements, women make statements sound like questions."

2 Using Expressions Find other examples of contrast expressions in the article. Underline them, and notice the way each fits grammatically into the sentence. Then combine the following sentences using a different contrast expression from the box in each.

in contrast	whereas
however	while
on the other hand	

1. Men tend to give advice. Women often show concern and empathy.

____

____

2. Women usually reveal a lot about their personal lives. Men rarely discuss personal relationships and feelings.

____

____

3. Women usually let speakers finish their sentences. Men tend to interrupt.

____

____

4. Men tend to be assertive in online communication. Women tend to hedge.

____

____

5. Men usually make declarative statements. Women often add question tags to the end of statements.

____

____

Paragraph Practice

3 Using New Words and Expressions Use the new words and expressions from this section to complete the following activities:

1. Look at the pairs of photos on page 46. In a paragraph, describe the behavior of the speakers in each pair. Use the contrast expressions taught in Activity 2 on page 52.
2. Rewrite your freewriting from Activity 6, page 50. Use the words and the expressions presented in this section.
3. In a paragraph, describe the communication style differences between the male and female characters in a play, movie, or TV program you saw for your research in Activity 7 on page 50. Use the words and expressions presented in this section.

Part 3 Organizing and Developing Your Ideas

Paragraph Development

Review Point

- A thesis statement previews an essay by presenting the writer's approach to the topic.

New Points

- The body paragraphs of an essay include specific facts and examples that illustrate the writer's approach to the topic.
- A well-developed body paragraph answers all the readers' questions about the topic.
- Writers create well-developed body paragraphs by anticipating readers' questions as they write.

ANTICIPATING READERS' QUESTIONS

Readers usually ask questions such as *Why*, *How*, *Who*, *What*, *Where*, and *When*? They often think to themselves:

- Explain more fully, please.
- Give an example, please.
- Prove it!

1 Studying a Well-Developed Paragraph Read the following well-developed paragraph and notice how the author anticipates and answers the readers' questions (in italics):

One way in which men's and women's speech differs is in the practice of interrupting. *(How?)* Studies have shown that men interrupt women much more often than they do other men, while women are less likely to interrupt either men or women. *(Prove it!)* At business meetings, for example, men typically engage in "competitive turn-taking," or grabbing the floor by interrupting another speaker. *(How are women different?)* Women, however, have been conditioned from childhood to believe that interrupting is impolite. *(Explain further, please.)* Instead, they sit for hours waiting for a turn to speak, while their male colleagues wonder if they'll ever have anything to say. *(What does this mean?)* This not only demonstrates a gender difference in speaking, it also illustrates one of the reasons that men and women do not understand each other.

—Georgia Dullea

How did the writer answer each of the readers' questions (shown in italics)? Find the details, examples, and explanations that answer each of the questions.

2 Analyzing a Paragraph Read the following paragraph. It is poorly developed because the writer did not anticipate the readers' questions and answer them. Try to answer the readers' questions (in italics) yourself, and then, on a separate piece of paper, rewrite the paragraph, developing it more fully.

One way to learn a foreign language is to watch the nonverbal communication of native speakers. *(Why?)* Watch how people behave when they talk to each other. *(Why?)* Observe the gestures they use and try to figure out what they mean. *(Give an example.)* You can learn many things about people just by watching their behavior as they speak. *(Why? What does this have to do with everything else you've said?)*

3 **Improving a Paragraph** The writer of the following paragraph did not anticipate possible questions the reader might have. Read the paragraph, then list the questions that a reader might ask after each sentence. Then rewrite the paragraph on a separate piece of paper. As you rewrite, improve it by answering the questions that you listed.

There are three areas of difference between men and women's communication styles. *(Question #1)* One area is using language to dominate, versus using it to establish rapport. *(Question #2)* Another area is in the use of declarative statements versus questions. *(Question #3)* Using and tolerating insults reflects another area of difference. *(Question #4)*

Question #1: ______________________________

Question #2: ______________________________

Question #3: ______________________________

Question #4: ______________________________

4 Writing a Well-Developed Paragraph Write a paragraph about the communication differences between males and females. As you write, record the questions a reader might ask on a separate piece of paper. Try to answer them in your paragraph. When you finish, exchange paragraphs with a partner. Evaluate your partner's paragraph by asking questions about each sentence. Write down any questions that the writer did not answer. Then compare your questions with the ones that your partner wrote while he or she was working on the paragraph.

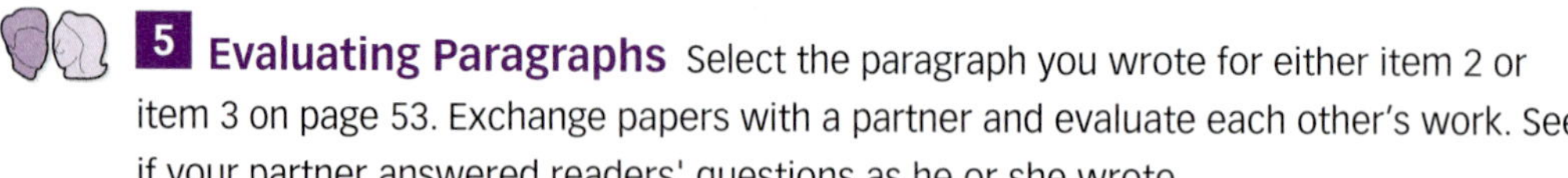

5 Evaluating Paragraphs Select the paragraph you wrote for either item 2 or item 3 on page 53. Exchange papers with a partner and evaluate each other's work. See if your partner answered readers' questions as he or she wrote.

TOEFL® IBT

Focus on Testing

Pretending That You Are the Reader

Activity 4 asks you to write a paragraph and then list possible reader questions about it. Pretending you are the reader as you write is a good strategy for an essay-test situation. Anticipate the questions your reader might have about each statement you write. If your statements answer all possible questions, you've written a well-developed paragraph or essay.

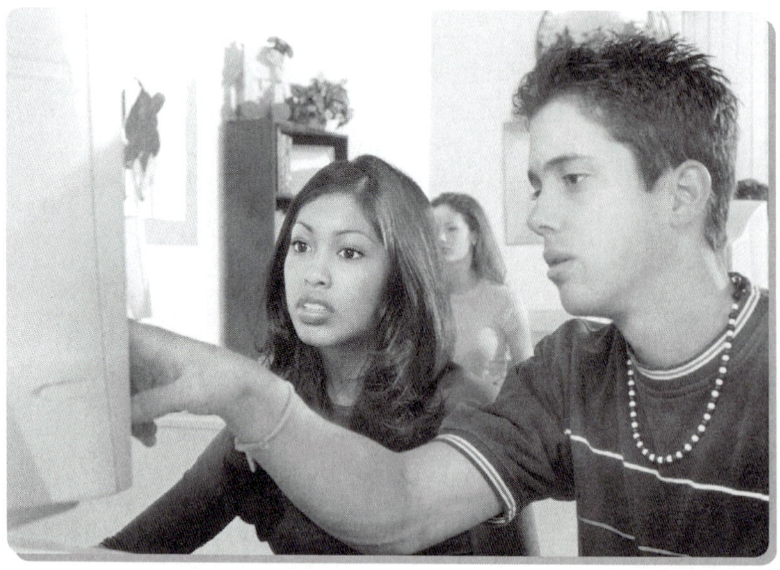

▲ Working with a partner on a piece of writing

Writing Product

6 Writing about Communication Styles Write an essay on the following topic:

Compare the communication style differences between men and women in your native language. Focus on one or more of the following:

Directness versus indirectness
Assertiveness versus unassertiveness
Tendency to interrupt
Body language
Word choice
Tag questions
Loudness
Conversation topic choice
Boasting/bragging
Dominating the conversation
Swearing
Insulting
Arguing

Use the ideas that you've discussed and written about so far in this chapter. Also, remember to:

- Use contrast words and expressions and the vocabulary you learned.
- Make sure your body paragraphs include specific facts and examples that illustrate your approach to the topic.
- Answer your readers' questions about the topic.

Part 4 Evaluating Your Writing

Use the following rubric to score your writing. Read over the rubric with your class, then give your writing a score. A classmate and a teacher will score your writing also and explain reasons for their scores.

If you want to revise and improve this essay or a piece of writing from a previous chapter, you can do it now.

Rubric for Writing About Gender Differences in Communication

Score	Description
3 **Excellent**	▪ **Content:** Writing presents one or more differences in communication styles between men and women and develops a complete description through examples, experiences, reasons, and/or statistics. ▪ **Organization:** Ideas are organized to support and explain main idea through an introduction, a main idea, body paragraphs, and a conclusion; ideas follow a logical sequence and are easy to follow. ▪ **Vocabulary and Sentence Structure:** Vocabulary is specific and descriptive; sentence types are varied. ▪ **Grammar:** Subjects and verbs agree; common grammar problems (pronouns, articles, and plurals) are minimal so that meaning is clear. ▪ **Spelling and Mechanics:** Most words are spelled correctly and punctuation is correct.
2 **Adequate**	▪ **Content:** Writing presents at least one difference in communication styles between men and women and describes the difference through one or more of the following ways: examples, experiences, reasons, or statistics. ▪ **Organization:** Ideas are organized and there is a clear beginning, middle, and end; main idea is clear; some parts may be undeveloped. ▪ **Vocabulary and Sentence Structure:** Vocabulary is descriptive; sentences are mostly the same type. ▪ **Grammar:** Subjects and verbs mostly agree; common grammar problems (pronouns, articles, and plurals) are distracting. ▪ **Spelling and Mechanics:** Some distracting spelling and/or punctuation mistakes exist.

1 **Developing**	■ **Content:** Writing does not present a difference in communication styles between men and women clearly or does not develop difference with sufficient description or detail. ■ **Organization:** Ideas do not follow essay format and are confusing or too brief. ■ **Vocabulary and Sentence Structure:** Vocabulary is limited and/or there are too many mistakes to understand and/or follow the ideas; sentences have mistakes. ■ **Grammar:** Many common grammar problems (pronouns, articles, and plurals) that are confusing to the reader. ■ **Spelling and Mechanics:** There are many distracting spelling and/or punctuation mistakes.

Self-Assessment Log

In this chapter, you worked through the following activities. How much did each of them help you become a better writer? Check *A lot*, *A little*, or *Not at all*.

	A lot	A little	Not at all
I discussed photos of women and men communicating.	❑	❑	❑
I read about gender differences in communication.	❑	❑	❑
I discussed gender differences in communication with my classmates.	❑	❑	❑
I recognized supporting information from experts.	❑	❑	❑
I studied words for writing about differences.	❑	❑	❑
I developed paragraphs by answering readers' questions.	❑	❑	❑
I evaluated my essay.	❑	❑	❑
(Add something) ______________________________ ______________________________	❑	❑	❑

Chapter 4

Beauty and Aesthetics

In This Chapter

Genre Focus: Cause and Effect

Writing Product

In this chapter, you'll write about personal aesthetics.

Writing Process

- Discuss photos of people who have changed or enhanced their natural appearance.
- Read about the history of tattoos.
- Use a timeline.
- Gather information about an aspect of personal aesthetics.
- Learn and use vocabulary for discussing the history of personal aesthetics.
- Use different types of supporting material.

"Everything has its beauty, but not everyone sees it."

—Confucius
Chinese philosopher (551–479 BCE)

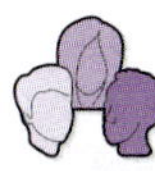

Connecting to the Topic

1. What makes people look attractive?
2. What doesn't make people look attractive?
3. How important to you is appearance?

Part 1 Preparing to Write

Getting Started

1 Discussing Personal Aesthetics Since the beginning of human history, people have been interested in changing or enhancing their appearance. Look at the following photos and discuss the ways in which the people in the photos have changed or enhanced their natural appearance.

▲ Modern formal wear

▲ Kabuki actors

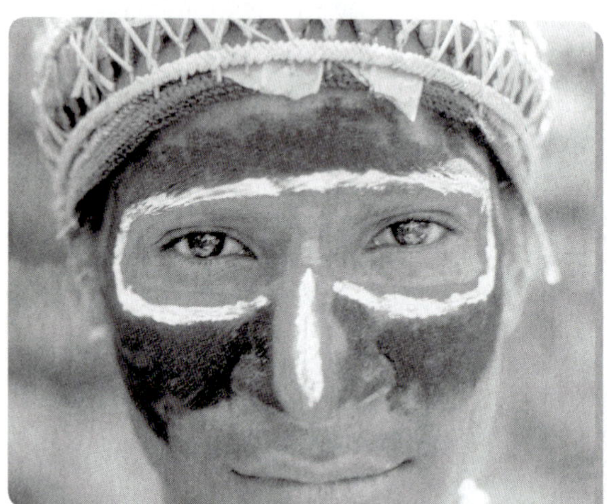

▲ Traditional face paint in Papua New Guinea

▲ *Mehndi* (hennaed hands)

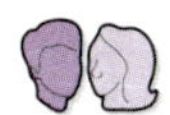

2 **Identifying Personal Choices** Why do people change or enhance their natural appearance? Below are a few reasons that anthropologists have identified; add your own ideas to this list. Then, discuss this question with a partner: Which of these reasons match the photos on page 62? When you are done, discuss the questions that follow.

- To enhance beauty
- To hide flaws
- To indicate one's place in a group or in society
- To indicate that one is of a certain age, e.g., adult as opposed to child
- To indicate wealth
- To disguise oneself or to become someone else
- To protect oneself from the environment
- Other ideas: ______________________________

1. How important is your appearance?

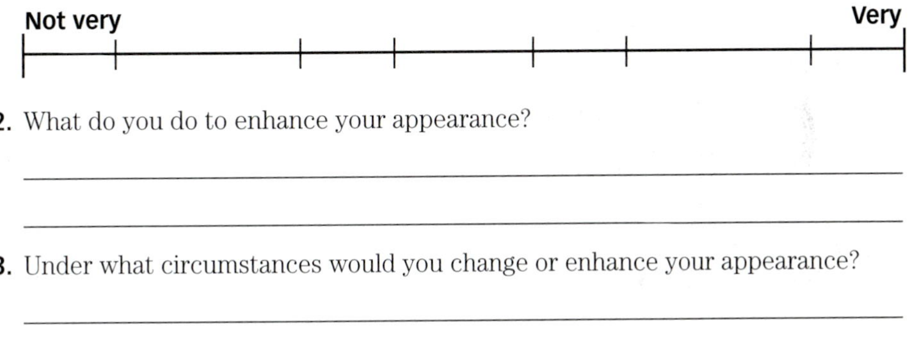

2. What do you do to enhance your appearance?

____

____

3. Under what circumstances would you change or enhance your appearance?

____

____

3 **Preparing to Read** On pages 64–66 is an article from National Geographic Online. The passage discusses the history of tattooing in different cultures around the world. Before you read, discuss these questions in small groups.

1. Many countries and cultures have a history of tattooing, including Tahiti, New Zealand, Hawaii, Japan, Egypt, ancient Rome, and certain Native American cultures of the Pacific Northwest. Find the locations of these cultures on the map on the next page and label them.

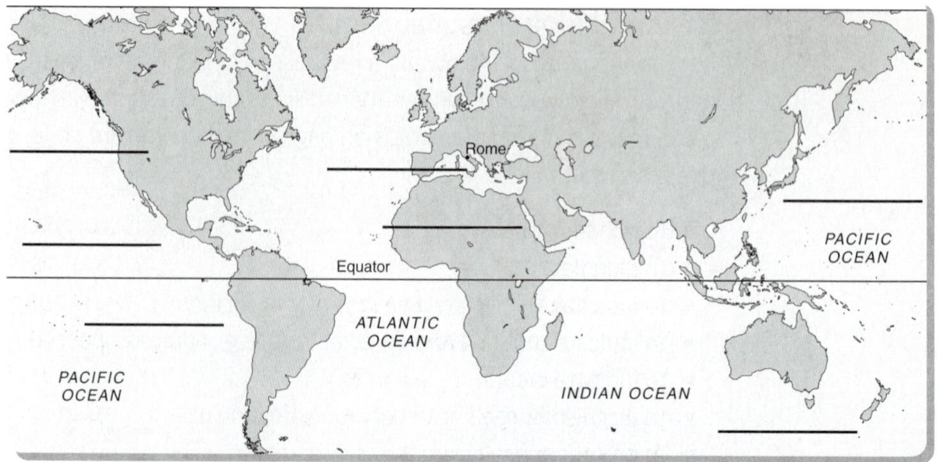

2. How do you think tattoos are applied today? How might they have been applied in the past?

____

____

3. What are some positive or negative attitudes that people have or had about tattooing?

____

____

4. What is your opinion of tattoos? Do you find them attractive? Why or why not?

____

____

Tattoos Across Time and Place

A “It’s a permanent reminder of a temporary feeling,” sings Jimmy Buffett about some parents’ dismay over their daughter’s tattoo. Yet those indelible body markings are more than a trend embraced by merchant marines, bikers, and goths in basic black. Tattoos arise from a rich cultural history dating back 5,000 years.

▲ Body tattoos

B The earliest example of tattoos so far discovered was found in 1991 on the frozen remains of the Copper Age "Iceman" scientists have named Ötzi. His lower back, ankles, knees, and a foot were marked with a series of small lines, made by rubbing powdered charcoal into vertical cuts. X-rays revealed bone degeneration at the site of each tattoo, leading researchers to believe that Ötzi's people, ancestors of contemporary central and northern Europeans, may have used tattoos as medical treatment to reduce pain.

C As civilizations developed, tattoos took on other meanings. Egyptian funerary figures of female dancers from around 2000 BCE, display the same abstract dot-and-dash tattoos on their bodies as those found on female mummies from the same time period. Later images represent Bes, god of fertility and revelry.

D Ancient Romans found no reason to celebrate tattoos, believing in the purity of the human form. Except as brands for criminals and the condemned, tattoos were banned in Rome. But over time, Roman attitudes toward tattoos changed. Fighting an army of Britons who wore their tattoos as badges of honor, some Romans came to admire their enemies' ferocity as well as the symbols they wore. Soon Roman soldiers were wearing their own body marks; Roman doctors even perfected the art of application and removal.

E During the Crusades of the eleventh and twelfth centuries, warriors identified themselves with the mark of the Jerusalem cross so that they could be given a proper Christian burial if they died in battle. After the Crusades, tattooing largely disappeared in the West for a time, but continued to flourish in other places.

F By the early eighteenth century, European sailors encountered the inhabitants of the South and Central Pacific islands. There, tattoos were an important part of the culture. When in mourning, Hawaiians tattooed their tongues with three dots. In Borneo, natives tattooed an eye on the palm of their hands as a spiritual guide that would lead them to the next life.

G In 1769, Captain James Cook landed in Tahiti, where the word "tattoo" originated from *tatau*, which means "to tap the mark into the body." One method island practitioners used for working their designs into the skin was with a razor-edged shell attached to the end of a stick. In New Zealand, Maori leaders signed treaties by drawing precise replicas of their *moko*, or personal facial tattoo. Such designs are still used to identify the wearer as a member of a certain family and to symbolize a person's achievements in life.

H Tattooing has been practiced in Japan—for beautification, magic, and to mark criminals—since around the fifth century BC. Repressive laws gave rise to the exquisite Japanese designs known today. Restricted from wearing the ornate kimonos that adorned royalty and the elite, outraged merchants and the lower classes rebelled by wearing tattooed body suits. Covering their torsos with illustrations that began at the neck and extended to the elbow and above the knee, wearers hid the intricate designs beneath their clothing. Viewing the practice as subversive, the government outlawed tattoos in 1870 as it entered a new era of international relationships. As a result, tattooists went underground, where the art flourished as an expression of the wearer's inner longings and impulses.

I The *yakuza*, the Japanese gangster class, embraced the body suits—even more so because they were illegal. Their elaborate designs usually represented an unresolved conflict and also included symbols of character traits the wearer wanted to emulate. A carp represented strength and perseverance. A lion stood for courage. Such tattoos required long periods of pain caused by the artist's bundles of needles, endured by wearers as a show of allegiance to their beliefs. Today, Japanese tattoo wearers are devoted to the most colorful, complete, and exotic expression of the art.

J New York inventor Samuel O'Reilly patented the first electric tattoo machine in 1891, making traditional tools a thing of the past in the West. By the end of the 1920s, American circuses employed more than 300 people with full-body tattoos who could earn an unprecedented $200 per week.

K For the next 50 years, tattoos gained a reputation as a mark of American fringe cultures, sailors, and World War II veterans. But today, tattoo connoisseurs take the spotlight at international fairs and conventions with Japanese body suits, Celtic symbols, black tribal motifs, and portraits of favorite celebrities.

L "Tattooing is enjoying a big renaissance around the world," says Chuck Eldridge of the Tattoo Archive in Berkeley, California. "Native American women in the Northwest are wearing chin tattoos again, reviving a cultural practice from centuries before the white man arrived. And, in answer to health concerns, artists in the South Pacific are slowly changing to modern equipment."

M "The melting pot that is the United States has no rites of passage as a single American culture," says Ken Brown, a tattoo artist in Fredericksburg, Virginia. "On some levels, getting a tattoo is like a milestone that marks a certain moment in a person's life." Ken still remembers one customer, an 80-year-old former marine who had always wanted a tattoo but had been too afraid to get one. "He came to me for his first tattoo," Ken says, "and he told me, 'I figure I got five or six good years left in me, and I'm not going out without one.'"

—Cassandra Franklin-Barbajosa, "Tattoo: Pigments of Imagination."

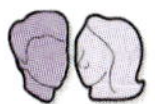

4 **Understanding the Reading** In small groups, answer the following questions.

1. How old is the practice of tattooing?

____

____

2. Where did the word *tattoo* come from?

____

____

3. Why did the Britons wear tattoos?

____

____

4. How did the Romans change their minds about tattoos?

____

____

5. What is the purpose of a *moko?*

____

____

6. Explain in your own words why modern Japanese tattoos are so intricate.

____

____

7. What is one way that tattoos were probably applied in the past? How are they applied today?

____

____

8. What might be one purpose of tattoos in modern American culture, according to Ken Brown?

____

____

Strategy

Thinking Critically: *Using a Timeline*

A timeline is a type of graphic organizer. It's a tool to help you keep track of events in history. You can use it to list who did what at particular points in time. A timeline can be horizontal or vertical and it contains dates and facts relevant to the dates. The dates go left-to-right or top-to-bottom. For example:

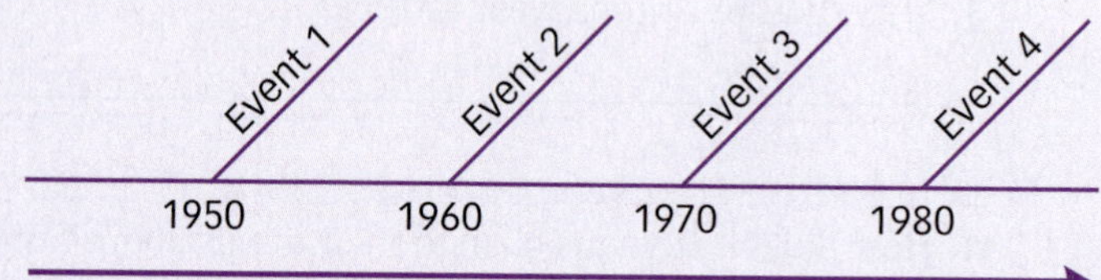

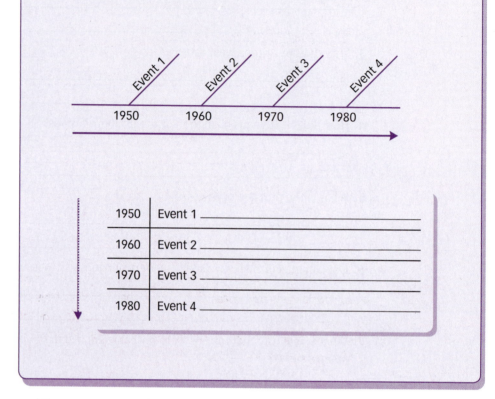

1950	Event 1 ______________________
1960	Event 2 ______________________
1970	Event 3 ______________________
1980	Event 4 ______________________

5 **Using a Timeline** Complete the following vertical timeline to record important facts from "Tattoos Across Time and Place." For each time period, indicate the cultures that have a history of tattooing, who used tattoos in those cultures, and examples or purposes of tattooing in the culture. Some have been done for you.

Time Period	Culture	Who?	What or Why?
Copper Age	Central/Northern Europe	Ötzi	to reduce pain
	Egypt	female dancers	symbols of Bes–god of fertility

6 **Freewriting** How important is appearance to you? Under what circumstances would you change your appearance? Under what circumstances do you try to look your best? How much time, money, and energy do you spend on changing or enhancing your appearance? Write for 15 minutes about your attitude toward personal aesthetics, either for yourself or for other people.

7 **Gathering Information** Choose an aspect of personal aesthetics from the list below that interests you, then follow the directions at the top of page 70.

- Facial hair (beard, mustaches)
- Hairstyles
- Clothing
- Accessories (neckties, shoes, hats, jewelry)
- Plastic surgery
- Cosmetics
- Body painting or piercing
- Body building
- Dieting
- Your own idea: ______________________________

Find someone who has the same interest. Work together to find out as much as you can about the history of the topic that you chose. Do library or Internet research. As you read, use a timeline similar to the one on page 68 to record important facts about your topic. Look for and make copies of pictures that illustrate your topic.

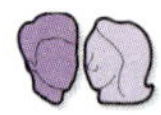

8 Sharing Results With your partner, give a presentation on the history of the topic that you researched. Use notes from your timeline and bring in any pictures that you found.

Part 2 Focusing on Words and Phrases

Discussing the History of Personal Aesthetics

1 Finding Meaning in Context Below are some words and expressions from "Tattoos Across Time and Place" on pages 64–66. Find them in the passage. Notice their contexts—how they are used in a sentence—and try to guess their meanings. Then match the meanings below to the words and expressions. Write the letters on the lines.

Words and Expressions	Meanings
___ **1.** abstract (Line 19)	**a.** impossible to remove
___ **2.** show of allegiance to (Line 67)	**b.** copy
___ **3.** badges of honor (Line 26)	**c.** fierceness
___ **4.** condemned (Lines 23–24)	**d.** cultures that are outside of the dominant one
___ **5.** emulate (Line 62)	**e.** statement
___ **6.** endured (Line 64)	**f.** nonrepresentational
___ **7.** ferocity (Line 26)	**g.** rebellious
___ **8.** fringe cultures (Line 72)	**i.** show of loyalty
___ **9.** indelible (Lines 4–5)	**j.** detailed
___ **10.** intricate (Line 54)	**k.** signs indicating achievement or status
___ **11.** expression (Line 58)	**l.** sentenced to die
___ **12.** subversive (Line 55)	**m.** experienced with difficulty

Below are some expressions from "Tattoos Across Time and Place" useful for discussing events in the past or the history of a cultural practice.

Noun Phrases

a cultural practice
a rich cultural history
rite(s) of passage
the earliest record of + NOUN

Verb Phrases

arise(s) from + NOUN
came to + VERB
dating back + NUMBER + years
gave rise to + NOUN . . . known today

Examples:

The melting pot that is the United States has no rites of passage as a single American culture.

Tattoos arise from a rich cultural history.

2 Using Expressions

Find the expressions in the list above in "Tattoos Across Time and Place" on pages 64–66, and notice how each fits into a sentence. Then complete the following sentences with the correct expression:

1. At first, Mark's parents were upset by his new tattoo; later, they ________________ accept it.
2. Mark got his first tattoo when he joined the army. Getting a tattoo was just one of many ________________ that Mark experienced when he joined the military.
3. Mark's parents learned that tattoos have a ________________. They were surprised that tattoos have been around for many years in many different civilizations.
4. Tattooing was an important ________________ among the inhabitants of South Pacific islands such as the Maori, who used it to symbolize life achievements.
5. ________________ of the use of lipstick was found in Babylon over 5,000 years ago.
6. The use of cosmetics isn't new; it ________________ from a rich cultural history.
7. Like cosmetics, plastic surgery comes from a long tradition ________________ thousands of years. For example, archaeologists have found evidence of the practice of plastic surgery in ancient Egypt.
8. Developments in medical techniques ________________ to the types of plastic surgery that we know today.

Paragraph Practice

3 Using New Words and Expressions Use the new words and expressions learned in this section to complete the following activities:

1. Using words and expressions from this section, write one paragraph about the history of the topic you chose in Activity 7 on page 69.
2. In your opinion, are tattoos ugly or beautiful? Express your opinion in one paragraph. Use words and expressions from this section.
3. Rewrite your Freewriting Activity from Part 1 using the words and expressions on pages 70-71.

Part 3 Organizing and Developing Your Ideas

Types of Supporting Material

Review Point

- A well-developed paragraph anticipates the readers' questions and answers them.

New Points

A well-developed paragraph includes a good amount of supporting material. The types of supporting material that writers usually use to develop their ideas include examples, facts, statistics, and anecdotes.

- An **example** is a representative person, quality, or event. It shows a common quality or illustrates a general rule.
- A **fact** is a piece of information that is true or an event that has happened. Facts record and present evidence.
- A **statistic** is a number or part of a collection of numbers that represent measurements or facts.
- An **anecdote** is a short story about a person or event that illustrates or dramatizes a point.

EXAMPLES OF SUPPORTING MATERIAL

Note the use of the above examples of supporting material in the following paragraph about the history of neckties:

Some aspects of contemporary men's fashion can be traced to ancient times. The necktie is just one example. **[Example]** In fact, the history of neckties dates back to the Roman Empire. Roman legionnaires wore a *focale,* a piece of cloth around their neck in order to keep warm. In the seventeenth century, a regiment from Croatia (then part of the Austro-Hungarian Empire) visited Paris and was presented to the king, Louis XIV. The officers of this regiment were wearing brightly colored handkerchiefs made of silk around their necks. **[Anecdote]** Louis XIV, well known for his interest in personal adornment, admired these neck cloths. He made them fashionable in France and even established a royal tie maker. The origins of this early version of the necktie remain in the French word for tie, *cravate,* which is derived from the word "Croat." **[Fact]** In twentieth century America, Jesse Langsdorf patented the long, pointed tie still popular today. And in spite of the trend toward casual business dress, necktie sales in the twenty-first century are booming, with some manufacturers reporting a 50 percent increase in sales in 2003 over the previous year. **[Statistic]**

1 Analyzing Examples of Supporting Material

Review the passage "Tattoos across Time and Place" on pages 64-66. Try to locate as many different types of supporting material as you can. State whether each piece of supporting material is an *example, a fact, a statistic,* or an *anecdote.* Use the following chart to record your findings.

Supporting Material from "Tattoos Across Time and Place"	Type: Example, Fact, Statistic, or Anecdote
New York inventor Samuel O'Reilly patented the first electric tattoo machine in 1891	fact
Japanese merchants and lower classes rebelled against. not being allowed to wear ornate kimonos by getting full-body tattoos	anecdote
American circuses employed 300 people w/full-body tattoos in late 1920s	statistic

Notice that it's not necessary to use each type of support in a paragraph. In fact, writers may sometimes only use examples to develop a main idea. In other cases, writers may want to provide statistics to convince readers of their main point. The type or types of supporting material depends on the main idea and the type of support that is available.

2 Identifying Types of Supporting Material Identify the main type(s) of supporting material in the following paragraphs and give two examples from each paragraph.

Many biologists agree that appearance results from both heredity and environment. A study of twins, Lisa and Lori, serves as an example of this. When they were children, people couldn't tell Lisa and Lori apart. However, as adults they look quite different. Even though they are genetically identical, Lisa looks much older than Lori. Lisa has deep lines in her face, while Lori's skin is smooth and youthful looking. Their personal histories serve as an explanation. Like many identical twins, they had similar life experiences: Both had three children, divorced after eight years of marriage, and both worked as nurses. However, Lisa lived in California, spent a lot of time in the sun, and smoked a pack of cigarettes every day. Lori, on the other had, lived in Pennsylvania, avoided the sun, and never smoked.

Main Type(s) of Supporting Material:

____

Examples:

____

____

____

Men are increasingly availing themselves of plastic surgery to enhance their appearance. More than 1.2 million men had cosmetic plastic surgery in 2004, representing 13 percent of the total cosmetic plastic surgery population. The number of males having cosmetic plastic surgery procedures increased 16 percent from 2000 to 2004. Nose reshaping was the most popular surgical cosmetic procedure for men in 2004, with 109,971 operations performed. Hair transplantation was the second most popular procedure. Forty-three thousand fifty-four procedures were performed in 2004, a 54 percent increase since 2000. Top cosmetic procedures for men in 2004 also included eyelid surgery, liposuction, and breast reduction.

—The American Society of Plastic Surgeons, 2004 Gender Quick Facts: Cosmetic Procedures.

Main Type(s) of Supporting Material:

____

Examples:

____

____

____

3 **Using Different Types of Supporting Material** Rewrite your freewriting from Activity 6 on page 69 using at least two different types of supporting material.

4 **Organizing Supporting Material** Look at the notes you collected for your presentation in Activity 8 on page 70. Use the following chart to put the information you collected in your research into the following categories: *examples, facts, statistics,* and *anecdotes.* Then decide if you have enough material to write about your topic. Collect more material if necessary, and add it to the chart below. This will help you write your essay for this chapter.

Topic: ____

Examples	Facts	Statistics	Anecdotes

TOEFL® IBT

Focus on Testing

Examples, Details, and Reasons

Part 3 of this chapter discusses kinds of supporting material. Prompts for the independent task in the TOEFL® iBT often tell you exactly what kinds of support you should use—examples, details, or reasons. Note that the word *or* indicates that you are allowed to use any or all of these kinds of support.

Examples are often useful when you want to describe possible situations or to name specific things that illustrate your point. *Details* can mean many things, from a brief description to a full outline of the steps in a process. Because the term means so many things, almost any response will contain *details*. *Reasons* tell why: why you believe your opinion is right, why someone should do something, etc.

Practice: Your choice of support type(s) will depend on the nature of the prompt. Look at the following sample prompts and circle one or more kinds of support you would be most likely to use. After you have finished, compare your choices with those of one or two other students.

The first item is done for you as an example.

1. Do you agree or disagree with the following statement: "Teachers are like a second set of parents"? Support your point of view with specific examples, details, or reasons.

examples (circled) details (circled) reasons (circled)

2. Should a university student study what he or she is interested in or study what his or her parents or advisers recommend? Support your point of view with specific examples, details, or reasons.

examples details reasons

3. Some people believe that it is good for students to wear uniforms (a required style of clothing). Others believe uniforms are bad for students. What do you believe about uniforms? Support your point of view with specific examples, details, or reasons.

examples details reasons

4. Describe an experience in which the behavior of a famous person—a sports star, a movie star, a politician, etc.—inspired you. Support your point of view with specific examples, details, or reasons.

examples details reasons

5. Do you agree or disagree with the following statement: "When one door closes, another opens"? Support your point of view with specific examples, details, or reasons.

examples details reasons

6. Some people believe that it is good to take three or four months off from studying—usually in the summer. Others believe that these vacations are a waste of time. What do you believe about school vacations? Support your point of view with specific examples, details, or reasons.

examples details reasons

Writing Product

6 Writing about Personal Aesthetics Write an essay on the following topic:

Write about the history of one aspect of personal aesthetics. You can write about the same topic that you researched and presented in Part 1 or a new one.

- Facial hair (beard, mustaches)
- Hairstyles
- Clothing
- Accessories (neckties, shoes, hats, jewelry)
- Plastic surgery
- Cosmetics
- Body painting or piercing
- Body building
- Dieting
- Your own idea: ______________________________

Use the ideas that you've discussed and written about so far in this chapter. Also, remember to develop the ideas in your body paragraphs with examples, facts, statistics, and anecdotes.

Part 4 Evaluating Your Writing

Use the following rubric to score your writing. Read the rubric with your class, then give your writing a score. A classmate and a teacher will score your writing also and explain reasons for their scores. If you want to revise this essay, you can do it now or wait until Chapter 6.

Rubric for Writing About Personal Aesthetics

Score	Description
3 **Excellent**	■ **Content:** Writing presents one aspect of personal aesthetics and explains its history completely through facts, examples, experiences, and/or statistics. ■ **Organization:** Ideas are organized to support and explain main idea through an introduction, a main idea, body paragraphs, and a conclusion; ideas follow a logical sequence and are easy to follow. ■ **Vocabulary and Sentence Structure:** Vocabulary is specific and descriptive; sentence types are varied. ■ **Grammar:** Subjects and verbs agree; common grammar problems (pronouns, articles, and plurals) are minimal so that meaning is clear. ■ **Spelling and Mechanics:** Most words are spelled correctly and punctuation is correct.
2 **Adequate**	■ **Content:** Writing presents one aspect of personal aesthetics and explains history, although reader may still have questions. ■ **Organization:** Ideas are organized and there is a clear beginning, middle, and end; main idea is clear; some parts may be undeveloped. ■ **Vocabulary and Sentence Structure:** Vocabulary is descriptive; sentences are mostly the same type. ■ **Grammar:** Subjects and verbs mostly agree; common grammar problems (pronouns, articles, and plurals) are distracting. ■ **Spelling and Mechanics:** Some distracting spelling and/or punctuation mistakes.

1 **Developing**	▪ **Content:** Writing does not present one aspect of personal aesthetics or explain history sufficiently. ▪ **Organization:** Ideas do not follow essay format and are confusing or too brief. ▪ **Vocabulary and Sentence Structure:** Vocabulary is limited and/or there are too many mistakes to understand and/or follow the ideas; sentences have mistakes. ▪ **Grammar:** Many common grammar problems (pronouns, articles, and plurals) that are confusing to the reader. ▪ **Spelling and Mechanics:** Many distracting spelling and/or punctuation mistakes.

Self-Assessment Log

In this chapter, you worked through these activities. How did each of them help you become a better writer? Check *A lot*, *A little*, or *Not at all*.

	A lot	**A little**	**Not at all**
I discussed photos of people who have changed or enhanced their natural appearance.	❑	❑	❑
I read about the history of tatoos.	❑	❑	❑
I discussed personal aesthetics with my classmates.	❑	❑	❑
I learned words for discussing the history of personal aesthetics.	❑	❑	❑
I learned to use a timeline.	❑	❑	❑
I learned to use different types of supporting material.	❑	❑	❑
I gathered information about an aspect of personal aesthetics.	❑	❑	❑
I evaluated my essay.	❑	❑	❑
(Add something) ______________________________	❑	❑	❑

____

Chapter 5

Transitions

In This Chapter

Genre Focus: Information

Writing Product

In this chapter, you'll write about a rite of passage.

Writing Process

- Discuss photos of rites of passage.
- Read about adulthood.
- Interpret a table.
- Interview someone about an important transition in his or her life.
- Learn and use vocabulary for writing about rites of passage.
- Organize and interpret supporting material in a paragraph.

"We have not passed that subtle line between childhood and adulthood until . . . we have stopped saying 'It got lost,' and say 'I lost it.'"

—Sydney J. Harris
American journalist (1917–1986)

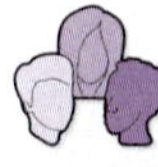

Connecting to the Topic

1. What does it mean to be an adult?
2. How does one become an adult?
3. What kind of transitions do you think are involved in becoming an adult?

Part 1 Preparing to Write

Getting Started

1 Discussing Rites of Passage Look at the photos. They illustrate rites of passage (ceremonies, rituals, or events that mark important changes, or transitions in a person's life). Then answer the questions that follow.

▲ Starting school (ages 5-6). The child's focus changes from inside the home to outside the home.

▲ Obtaining a driver's license (age 16-18). Being able to drive alone results in greater independence.

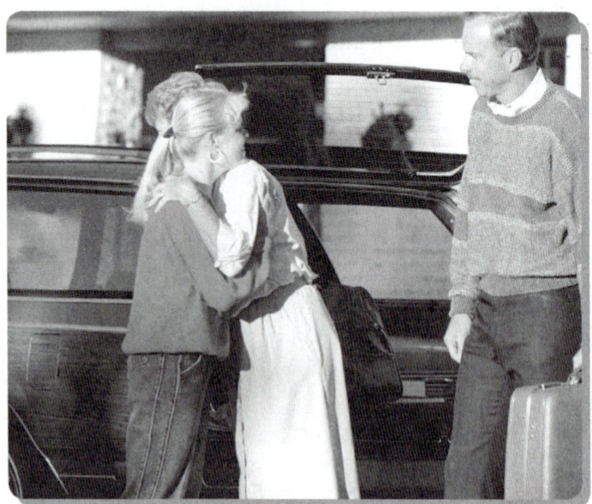

▲ Graduating from secondary school and starting college.

▲ Getting married. Responsibility extends to another person.

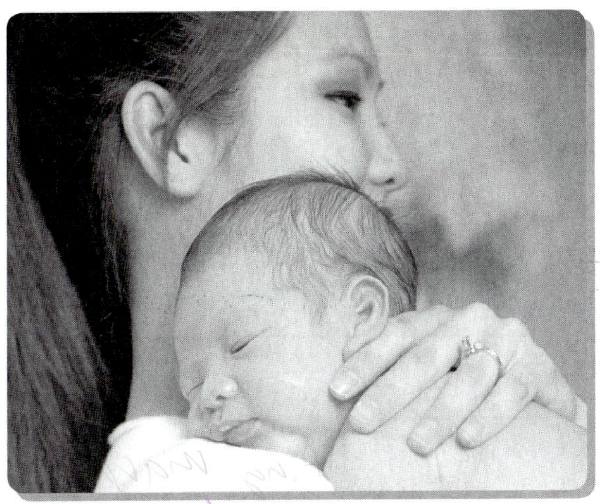

▲ Having children. Financial responsibilities increase.

▲ Retiring. The freedom to structure time as one chooses can be pleasurable or problematic.

1. Which rites of passage are related to becoming an adult?

marrige

getting married.

2. Which rites of passage give people more independence?

starting college

3. Which rites of passage give people more responsibility?

Having Children

4. How many of these rites of passage have you experienced? Which ones?

~~three~~ of them

two

1. 3

Vote

2 Brainstorming

Think of more rites of passage in your culture or in any culture you are familiar with. What are they called? At what age do people usually experience them? What is their purpose? Complete the following chart.

	Rite of Passage	Age	Purpose
Venezuela	Being 15	15	Girl → women
Korea	Drinking	19	get drunk
China	marry	men: 22 women: 20	getting marry
Korea	license	18	driving
Same	voting	18	to Vote for President.
	retirement	55–60	finish
Venezuela	College	17	get into College
〃	primary school	7	Start to Primary school

Now, compare your chart with the photos illustrating rites of passage in Activity 1. Discuss the differences and similarities with your classmates.

3 Preparing to Read

The passage on pages 85–86 is an excerpt from a college sociology textbook. Before you read, answer the following questions:

H.W

1. What does *adolescence* mean? What is another word for an *adolescent?*

___

___

2. What do you think most Americans would say is the key event that marks becoming an adult? What would most people from your culture say is the key event that marks becoming an adult?

___

___

3. How important are the following life events, in your opinion? Number them from 1 to 7, with 1 being the most important.

_____ Financial independence from parents/guardians

_____ Separate residence from parents

_____ Full-time employment

_____ Completion of formal schooling

_____ Capability of supporting a family

_____ Marriage

_____ Parenthood

4. Think about the elderly people that you know in your culture. Are they treated well? Are they happy with their lives? How active are they?

____

____

The Life Course

A Among the Kota people of the Congo in Africa, adolescents paint themselves blue. Mexican American girls go on a day-long religious retreat before dancing the night away. Egyptian mothers step over their newborn infants seven times, and students at the Naval Academy throw their hats in the air. These are all ways of celebrating rites of passage, a means of dramatizing and validating changes in a person's status.

B The Kota rite marks the passage to adulthood. The color blue, viewed as the color of death, symbolizes the death of childhood. Hispanic girls celebrate reaching womanhood with a *quinceañera* ceremony at age 15. In the Cuban American community of Miami [Florida], the popularity of the *quinceañera* supports a network of party planners, caterers, dress designers, and the Miss Quinceañera Latina pageant. For thousands of years, Egyptian mothers have welcomed their newborns to the world in the Sebou ceremony by stepping over the seven-day-old infant seven times. And Naval Academy seniors celebrate their graduation from college by hurling their hats skyward (D. Cohen 1991; Garza 1993; McLane 1995; Quadagno 2002).

▲ A *quinceañera* celebration.

▲ Freshman cadets at the Virginia Military Institute crawl up a muddy hill in a rite of passage at the school.

C These specific ceremonies mark stages of development in the life course. They indicate that the socialization process continues through all stages of the human life cycle. Sociologists and other social scientists use the life-course approach in recognition that biological conditions mold but do not dictate human behavior from birth until death.

D In the culture of the United States, each individual has a "personal biography" that is influenced by events both in the family and in the larger society. While the completion of religious confirmations, school graduations, marriage, and parenthood can all be regarded as rites of passage in a society, people do not necessarily experience them at the same time. The timing depends on such factors as one's gender, economic background, place of residence (central city, suburb, or rural area), and even time of birth.

E Several life events mark the passage to adulthood. Of course, these turning points vary from one society and even one generation to the next. According to a survey done in 2002, Americans view the end of formal schooling as the key event that marks becoming an adult. On average, most Americans expect this milestone to occur by age 23. Other major events in the life course, such as getting married or becoming a parent, are expected to follow three or four years later. Interestingly, most survey respondents did not view marriage and parenthood as important milestones.

F We encounter some of the most difficult socialization challenges (and rites of passage) in the later years of life. Assessing one's accomplishments, coping with declining physical abilities, experiencing retirement, and facing the inevitability of death may lead to painful adjustments. Old age is further complicated by the negative way that many societies view and treat the elderly. However, the common attitudes toward the elderly as helpless and dependent have undergone dramatic changes in recent decades. Increasingly, many older people continue to lead active, productive, fulfilled lives—whether in the paid labor force or as retirees.

—Adapted from Richard T. Schaefer, *Sociology,* Ninth Edition and *Sociology: A Brief Introduction,* Third Edition.

MILESTONES IN THE TRANSITION TO ADULTHOOD		
Life Event	**Expected Age**	**Percentage of People Who View Event as Extremely/Quite Important**
Financial independence from parents/guardians	20.9 years	80.9%
Separate residence from parents	21.1	57.2
Full-time employment	21.2	83.8
Completion of formal schooling	22.3	90.2
Capability of supporting a family	24.5	82.3
Marriage	25.7	33.2
Parenthood	26.2	29.0

Source: T. Smith. Based on a 2002 General Survey of 1,398 people.

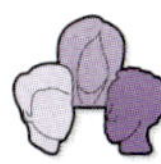

4 **Understanding the Reading** In small groups, do the following tasks and answer the following questions:

1. Give an example of a culture that clearly marks the difference between childhood and adulthood.

   ____

   ____

2. What do most Americans say is the key event that marks becoming an adult?

   ____

   ____

3. Which life event was considered to be the most important to Americans in a 2002 survey?

   ____

   ____

4. Do all people in a particular society tend to experience life events at the same time? Explain your answer and give an example.

   ____

   ____

5. Why does the author say: "We encounter some of the most difficult socialization challenges (and rites of passage) in the later years of life."?

   ____

   ____

Strategy

Thinking Critically: *Interpreting Tables*

Authors of academic and scientific material often show important information in tables and graphs. Tables and graphs can make it easy to see patterns and relationships in a great deal of information. They often contain information that you can use in your writing or that will appear on a test.

Information (or data) in tables is usually organized according to categories. These categories are presented horizontally and vertically, usually in bold type. To read a table, scan the title and the category heads. Then find specific information that appears where the horizontal and vertical categories connect. For example, here is a question about the information in the table on page 87: "At what age do most Americans expect a person to get married?" To find the answer, scan at the horizontal heads for "Expected Age." Then scan the vertical categories for "Marriage." The answer is 25.7 years old.

5 Practicing Reading Tables Use the table on page 87 to answer the following questions.

1. What percentage of people view full-time employment as extremely or quite important?
2. What is the expected age of parenthood?
3. What percentage of people view parenthood as extremely or quite important?
4. What percentage of people view marriage as extremely or quite important?
5. What is the expected age for people to complete formal schooling?

6 Freewriting Choose a rite of passage from a culture you are familiar with and write about it for 15 minutes without stopping. Include as much information as you can about the event: the age of the person, the purpose of the rite of passage, and details such as what people do during the event.

7 Gathering Information Collect information on a rite of passage from a culture that interests you by interviewing someone from that culture. You may consider religious and ethnic rites of passage—for example, confirmation, *bar* or *bat mitzvah*, or *quinceañera*—or you can use the life events in the table on page 87. Before the interview, think of what you would like to know and write a questionnaire like the following:

Questionnaire About Life Transitions

1. Name of person interviewed: Rafael
2. Rite of passage: separate residence from parents
3. Sex: Male 4. Age at time of rite: 16
5. What does the rite of passage involve? What happens?
moving to U.S.
6. What is the person's status before the rite?
IEP student
7. What is the person's status after the rite?
get a good job
8. What is the purpose of this rite in this culture?
become an adult.
9. Additional information/comments:
it helps me to grow faster than usual.

8 Sharing Results Give a brief presentation on the rite of passage that you learned about. If possible, bring pictures, photos, music, or objects associated with the rite to make your presentation more interesting.

Part 2 Focusing on Words and Phrases

Discussing Rites of Passage

1 Finding Meaning in Context On page 90 are some words and expressions from "The Life Course" on pages 85–86. Find them in the passage. Notice their contexts—how they are used in a sentence—and try to guess their meanings. Then match the meanings below to the words and expressions. Write the letters on the lines. Note: Two words have the same meaning.

Words and Expressions	Meanings
____ 1. ceremony (Line 10)	a. the process of teaching someone to behave according to a group's rules or values
____ 2. mark (Line 7)	b. times when changes occur
____ 3. milestone (Line 47)	c. ritual
____ 4. rite (Line 7)	d. confirming
____ 5. socialization (Line 26)	e. place or rank in a group or organization
____ 6. status (Line 6)	f. an important event or point in time
____ 7. turning points (Line 44)	g. show; indicate
____ 8. validating (Line 6)	h. formal procedure

2 Using Expressions

Study these expressions for discussing rites of passage and important life events. Find them in "The Life Course" on pages 85–86 and notice how they are used in a sentence.

becoming an adult	financial independence
formal schooling	the life course
the human life cycle	the passage to adulthood
stages of development	supporting a family

Now complete each sentence with one of the expressions. More than one expression may be correct in some sentences.

1. ____________________ is clearly marked among the Kota people of the Congo. Adolescents paint themselves blue to show that they are no longer children.
2. Girls in certain Latin American communities in the United States mark ____________________ with large parties on their fifteenth birthday.
3. A large percentage of Americans view the end of ____________________ as the main event that marks adulthood.
4. Some cultures view ____________________ as an important life event. Others do not feel that supporting yourself without your parents' help is very significant.
5. All cultures have important events that mark transitions in ____________________. These celebrations often begin at birth and end at death.
6. ____________________—being able to take care of others as well as yourself—is considered to be an important milestone in some cultures.

Paragraph Practice

3 Using New Words and Expressions Use the new words and expressions from Part 2 to complete the following activities:

1. Write a paragraph about the rite of passage that you learned about from your interview in Activity 7 on page 88. Use as many of the words and expressions from this section as you can.
2. Rewrite your freewriting from Activity 6 on page 88, using words and expressions presented in this section.
3. Write a paragraph about adolescence in your culture. Concentrate on the changes that a person makes during this period, and use words and expressions from this section.

Part 3 Organizing and Developing Your Ideas

Organizing Supporting Material

Review Point

- You can use different kinds of supporting information to develop the main ideas of a paragraph: examples, facts, statistics, and anecdotes.
- You can use different types of support in one paragraph, or use the same kind.
- The type of support you choose depends on the main idea of your paragraph.

New Points

- A well-developed paragraph includes the following: a topic sentence, an optional bridge statement, supporting material, and a conclusion.
- These parts of a well-developed paragraph have the following purposes:
  1. The *topic sentence* expresses the main idea.
  2. The *bridge* explains the main idea and connects it to the supporting material.
  3. The *supporting material* includes examples, facts, statistics, or an anecdote.
  4. The *conclusion* reminds the reader of the main idea and concludes the paragraph.

1 Analyzing a Well-Developed Paragraph Read the following paragraph and identify its parts (topic sentence, bridge, supporting material, and conclusion) by answering the questions.

(1) Adolescents form a large and powerful group in North American society. (2) Teenagers, in the United States and Canada, receive a lot of attention because of their purchasing power. (3) They are important targets for advertisers of clothing companies, who introduce many fashions designed especially for teen taste and lifestyle. (4) Special magazines, books, and newspaper columns are also written only for teens. (5) The entertainment industry has a huge market in its vast audience of teenagers. (6) Finally, a variety of products are designed exclusively for young Americans between twelve and twenty. (7) It's clear that adolescents comprise an important and powerful market in North America.

What is Sentence 1? ____________________

What is Sentence 2? ____________________

What is Sentence 3? ____________________

What is Sentence 4? ____________________

What is Sentence 5? ____________________

What is Sentence 6? ____________________

What is Sentence 7? ____________________

Interpreting Supporting Material

New Points

- A well-developed paragraph often includes an interpretation (or analysis) of the supporting material.
- An interpretation is one or more sentences that follow the supporting material. It explains how the supporting material relates to and develops the topic sentence.

2 Studying an Example of Interpretation Read the paragraph on the next page and notice how the interpretation (underlined) connects the supporting material and the topic sentence.

Topic sentence — At age six, a child begins to separate herself from her family and to take her place as a responsible citizen of the

Bridge — outside world. This act of separating includes many changes

Example 1 — in behavior and attitude. She becomes more independent of

Example 2 — her parents and often can get impatient with them. She is more

Example 3 — concerned with what other children say and do. She becomes interested in impersonal subjects like arithmetic and insects.

Interpretation — The change in interest from parents and personal subjects to peers and less personal subjects is a clear indication of this movement toward independence. It is at six, then, that

Conclusion — that the path to self-sufficiency and adulthood begins.

3 Analyzing an Interpretation Paragraph Read the following paragraphs and identify the parts by labeling each sentence, as you saw in the previous paragraph.

In many cultures, the end of formal schooling marks the beginning of adulthood. It is at this time that young people assume adult responsibilities. For example, they move away from home and have their own domestic concerns. Also, they are often partly if not fully responsible for supporting themselves financially. Finally, they are expected to make their own decisions. Thus, the assumption of both personal and financial responsibilities is the true passage to adulthood. So it is at the end of formal schooling that young people in many cultures become adults.

The transition from middle to old age is a period of critical biological and social change for many people. Physical decline disrupts habitual activity, and retirement changes one's lifestyle dramatically. Because of the changes in social role, retirement can also bring new opportunities such as the chance to explore a new career or hobby. Changing attitudes toward the elderly in certain cultures has improved the lives of many people as they grow older. It is important to be aware of the importance of a society's attitudes toward its members as they make the transition from one social role to another.

4 Practicing What You've Learned Complete the following topic sentence and bridge sentence and think of some supporting examples for your topic sentence. Then use your topic sentence, bridge sentence, and supporting information to write a complete paragraph by adding supporting material, an interpretation, and a conclusion. Use the paragraph in Activity 1 on page 92 as a model.

- Topic sentence: For someone from my culture, the transition from adolescence to adulthood can occur ____ ____ (time or age).
- Bridge sentence: This is due to ____ ____ (reason the transition happens at this time or age).
- Supporting examples:
____
____
____
- Interpretation:
____
____
____
____
- Conclusion:
____
____

5 Applying What You've Learned Write a paragraph about a personal or social transition. Use all of the parts of a well-developed paragraph that you reviewed in this section.

TOEFL® IBT

Focus on Testing

Writing About Personal Transitions on Standardized Tests

This chapter has given you many tools for writing about transition points in your personal life. The TOEFL® iBT asks you to respond to two prompts: (1) an independent prompt and (2) an integrated prompt. Some independent prompts deal with transition points in life, much as this chapter does. A lot of the vocabulary you have learned in this chapter can be useful if you get such a question on the TOEFL® iBT.

Here is a sample TOEFL® iBT-like prompt about transitions:

Describe a problem you had during your school years and how it has affected your life. Use specific examples or reasons to support your description.

Note how this sample includes several features of a typical independent prompt on the TOEFL® iBT:

- It asks about a personal experience, preference, or opinion.
- It has a connection to an academic setting or situation.
- It asks not just for a description but also for an explanation of some aspect of the experience.

Practice: Using some of the "personal transition" vocabulary you have learned in this chapter, write a response to one of the following prompts. Set a timer so you spend no more than 30 minutes planning, writing, and revising your response.

Prompts:

1. Explain a difficult decision you had to make in order to do well in your studies. Support your explanation with specific examples, details, or reasons.
2. Describe a time when you succeeded academically. How did you react to your success? Support your response with specific examples, details, or reasons.
3. Everyone experiences disappointments in student life—a bad test score, an unfair comment from a teacher, the loss of a good friend at school, etc. Tell about one such disappointment you have experienced. Support your response with specific examples, details, or reasons.

Writing Product

6 Writing About a Rite of Passage Write an essay on the following topic, using the ideas that you've discussed and written about so far in this chapter.

Describe and analyze a rite of passage from your culture. Give examples when appropriate. Focus on one or more of the following:

- the purpose of the ritual
- what happens during the ritual
- what participants, do, wear, eat, and so on, during the ritual
- the person's status before and after the ritual
- additional information about the ritual

Part 4 Evaluating Your Writing

Use the following rubric to score your writing. Read the rubric with your class, then give your writing a score. A classmate and a teacher will score your writing also and explain reasons for their scores. If you want to revise and improve this essay or writing from a previous chapter, you can do it now.

Rubric for Writing About Rite of Passage

Score	Description
3 **Excellent**	■ **Content:** Writing presents a rite of passage and analyzes it completely through facts, examples, experiences, and/or anecdotes. ■ **Organization:** Ideas are organized to support and explain main idea through an introduction, a main idea, body paragraphs, and a conclusion; ideas follow a logical sequence and are easy to follow. ■ **Vocabulary and Sentence Structure:** Vocabulary is specific and descriptive; sentence types are varied. ■ **Grammar:** Subjects and verbs agree; common grammar problems (pronouns, articles, and plurals) are minimal so that meaning is clear. ■ **Spelling and Mechanics:** Most words are spelled correctly and punctuation is correct.
2 **Adequate**	■ **Content:** Writing presents a rite of passage and explains it, although reader may still have questions. ■ **Organization:** Ideas are organized and there is a clear beginning, middle, and end; main idea is clear; some parts may be undeveloped. ■ **Vocabulary and Sentence Structure:** Vocabulary is descriptive; sentences are mostly the same type. ■ **Grammar:** Subjects and verbs mostly agree; common grammar problems (pronouns, articles, and plurals) are distracting. ■ **Spelling and Mechanics:** There are some distracting spelling and/or punctuation mistakes.

1 Developing	■ **Content:** Writing does not present a rite of passage or explain it's history sufficiently. ■ **Organization:** Ideas do not follow essay format and are confusing or too brief. ■ **Vocabulary and Sentence Structure:** Vocabulary is limited and/or there are too many mistakes to understand and/or follow the ideas; sentences have mistakes. ■ **Grammar:** There are many common grammar problems (pronouns, articles, and plurals) that are confusing to the reader. ■ **Spelling and Mechanics:** There are many distracting spelling and/or punctuation mistakes.

Self-Assessment Log

In this chapter, you worked through these activities. How did each of them help you become a better writer? Check *A lot*, *A little*, or *Not at all*.

	A lot	A little	Not at all
I discussed photos of rites of passage.	❑	❑	❑
I read about adulthood.	❑	❑	❑
I learned how to interpret a table.	❑	❑	❑
I interviewed someone about an important transition in his or her life.	❑	❑	❑
I learned and used vocabulary for writing about rites of passage.	❑	❑	❑
I organized and interpreted supporting material in a paragraph.	❑	❑	❑
I evaluated my first draft.	❑	❑	❑
I evaluated my second draft.	❑	❑	❑
(Add something) ______________________________ ______________________________	❑	❑	❑

Chapter 6

The Mind

In This Chapter

Genre Focus: Analysis

Writing Product

In this chapter, you'll write about a dream.

Writing Process

- Discuss art that deals with dreams.
- Read about the meaning of dreams.
- Interpret symbols.
- Gather information about dreams.
- Learn and use vocabulary for writing about dreams.
- Organize paragraphs according to levels of generality.

"Why does the eye see a thing more clearly in dreams than the imagination when awake?"

—Leonardo da Vinci
Italian artist (1452–1519)

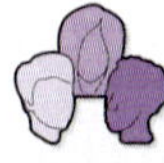

Connecting to the Topic

1. Why do you think people dream?
2. Do dreams have any meaning? Give examples.
3. What are some ways to interpret dreams?

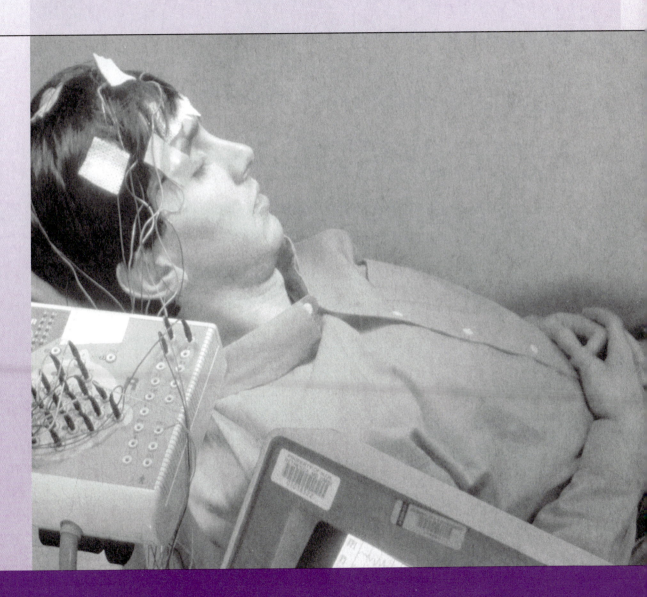

Part 1 Preparing to Write

Getting Started

1 Discussing Dreams What do our dreams mean? Are they important messages for the dreamer? The art on these pages deals with sleep and dreaming. Look at each picture, then answer the questions.

▲ *The Nightmare,* Henry Fuseli

▲ *The Dream of Reason Produces Monsters,* Francisco Goya

1. Describe the two pictures. How does the title of each match what you see in the picture?

   ____

   ____

2. What do you think the dreamers of these pictures are dreaming about?

   ____

   ____

3. Describe how each picture makes you feel. Do either of them remind you of a dream you've had?

   ____

   ____

2 Interviewing

Interview a partner by asking the following questions. Take notes on his/her responses.

1. When you dream, do you remember your dreams? yes no
2. Are your dreams in color or in black and white? color black/white
3. Can you remember different dreams you've had at different points in your life? yes no
4. Do you have any recurring dreams (dreams that you have over and over again)? What are they about? ______________________
5. Do you have any recurring themes or images in your dreams (such as water, animals, a house, etc.)? What are they? ______________________
6. Which of these common dream experiences have you had?
   a. being late for an important event
   b. losing a tooth
   c. flying
   d. falling
   e. being chased
   f. finding or losing valuables

3 Sharing Results

Now combine your answers with those of your classmates in a class survey. Can you draw any conclusions? For example:

- Are women more likely to remember their dreams than men?
- Are women more likely to dream in color?
- Are there any differences (in general) between men's and women's dreams?
- Do you share any dream images or themes with other students?
- Do you share any dream experiences with other students?

4 Preparing to Read

You are going to read a magazine article about recurring dreams and what they may mean. Answer the following questions before you read:

1. Have you ever tried to interpret a dream? How do people interpret dreams?
____
____
2. Who was Sigmund Freud? What did he say about dreams?
____
____

The Dream That Haunts You

A For years, Helen Thacker has had the same distressing dream. "I'm trapped in a dark tunnel with men standing at the entrance waiting to attack me. When I scream for help, no sound comes out. I try again. A whisper. Finally, with all the strength I have, I yell." Suddenly, she's awake. "I can't tell you how terrifying that dream is. Usually my heart pounds and my body's wet with sweat. Sometimes I'm upset all through the next day."

▲ Sigmund Freud

B Like Thacker, millions of people have recurring dreams that play inside their heads like scratched records. These dreams may be exhilarating—you fly down halls and over cities. Or they may be nightmares that jolt you into consciousness after you've been chased, yet again, by giant bugs, vampires, or men with guns. Often the dreams have traumatic plots that leave you feeling upset in the morning. In one study of women's dreams by Rosalind Cartwright, Ph.D., a psychology and social sciences professor at Chicago's Rush-Presbyterian-St. Luke's Medical Center, women describe nearly 50 percent of their recurring dreams as "highly unpleasant" and only 8 percent as "strongly pleasant."

C The ancient Greeks claimed dreams were messages from the gods. In the Middle Ages, dreams supposedly marked visits from demons. Late nineteenth-century doctors thought that nightmares came from difficulty breathing and a reduced oxygen supply to the brain. Contemporary theorists have their own explanations.

D Some scientists believe all dreams are a physiological response to our brain's nighttime activities. "They are simply our awareness of automatic activation of the brain during sleep," says J. Allen Hobson, M.D., a psychiatry professor at Harvard University and author of *The Dreaming Brain*. The brain stem sends signals to the cortex (the center of vision and thought), and the cortex turns those signals into dream stories. Your own experiences and emotions do contribute to the dream, however. Stored in your memory, they organize the story that you dream. "But dreaming is largely a random process," adds Dr. Hobson. "A lot of the nonsense of dreams is nonsense."

E Not so, say other experts, who view repeated dreams as messages from a person's deepest self, or the "royal road," as Freud wrote, to the unconscious. "Dreams offer an unfailing view of the conflicts within a person," contends Edward N. Brennan, M.D., an assistant professor of clinical psychiatry at Columbia University. And they present that view through metaphors and symbols.

G A woman who frequently dreams of being chased by men, for instance, may unconsciously want closeness to a man but be afraid. Until she masters her anxiety, her dreams will recur. Her response can be likened to a tongue probing the roof of a mouth burned by hot food: "The dream keeps saying, 'This is where it hurts,'" says Dr. Brennan. "And it will show you again and again and again."

H Occasionally, recurring dreams may even predict the future, says Stanley Krippner, Ph.D., a professor of psychology at San Francisco's Saybrook Institute and coauthor of *Dream Telepathy*. He tells of one woman who kept dreaming about a chandelier falling and crushing her baby in her crib. One night a clock in the dream said 2 a.m.. Frightened, the woman woke up and moved the baby to her own bed. At 2 a.m. the chandelier crashed.

I Of course, this mother may have unconsciously noted cracks in the ceiling plaster or the danger of her infant's sleeping below a chandelier. "The brain puts together a lot of little pieces of information and comes up with a [dream] conclusion that is sometimes very accurate," Dr. Krippner explains. But the dream clock's 2 a.m. went beyond her five senses' perceptions. The image was either precognition or just an educated guess.

J "Dreams look out for our best interests," says Dr. Krippner. In some cases they may even alert us to illness. In a study by Robert Smith, M.D., a professor of psychiatry at Michigan State University in East Lansing, when cardiac patients reported death and separation dreams, often recurring, their hearts were functioning poorly, but the patients did not know how sick they were.

K Recurring dreams can also give advice. Consider the "be prepared" message tucked into the recurring dream of Linda Jo Bartholomew, a Stanford University English lecturer: "I have a plane to catch, but instead of packing, I clean the sink or polish shoes. The dream always makes me feel terrible that I've planned so poorly," she admits.

L What do recurring dreams mean? It depends on you and how each symbol connects to your own life. Specific symbols have meanings unique to every dreamer. A bow and arrow in a dream, for example, may stand for persecution, but also for self-defense.

L Because of the intimate relationship between you and what you dream, "don't let anybody tell you what your dreams mean. Only you can know," says Gayle Delaney, Ph.D., author of *Breakthrough Dreaming*. To decipher them, she suggests writing a description of every image, then asking yourself: What real-life situation resembles this dream?

M Using that method, Iris McCarthy figured out a dream that recurred for five years: "I was crouching in my kitchen. When the police came around a side gate and saw me, they started shooting through the window. I could feel the bullets sinking in my flesh." Who were the police? "My mother-in-law," says McCarthy, a Mill Valley, California, housewife and mother of three. "Once, she did walk around my house, looking through windows for me. I was always trying to escape her wrath."

N When interpreting repetitive dreams, watch for common symbols. Clothing may indicate feelings about body image. Houses may represent your perception of your life. Cars, too, can reflect your life and whether you're going along smooth or bumpy "roads."

O Deborah Dembo, a pediatric nurse in Stanford, California, occasionally dreams that her Honda is trapped in water or on a steep incline: "I can't drive up higher or turn around and go back down. There's no way out." To her, the car symbolizes freedom and independence, and so the dream could mean something in her life is "stuck."

—Kristin von Kreisler

5 **Understanding the Reading** In small groups, answer these questions about "The Dream That Haunts You."

1. What are some beliefs about dreaming that people have had in the past?

____

____

2. What are two explanations for dreaming, according to the article?

____

____

3. State in your own words at least three purposes of recurring dreams, according to the article.

____

____

4. What is a possible explanation of the chandelier dream that supposedly predicted the future?

____

5. What do recurring dreams mean, according to the article?

____

____

6. How are we supposed to interpret recurring dream symbols, according to the article?

____

____

7. Do you agree with the article? Are there any other explanations for why people dream that aren't mentioned in the article?

____

____

Strategy

Thinking Critically: *Interpreting Symbols*

Post-reading Questions 4 and 6 ask you to look for additional meanings or explanations beyond the literal (accurate or exact) meanings of certain events or symbols. This is called *interpreting*. It is an important critical thinking skill.

6 Interpreting Dream Symbols Practice interpreting the dream symbols below. Then think of additional dream symbols and suggest interpretations for them. Use the following graphic organizer to record your ideas.

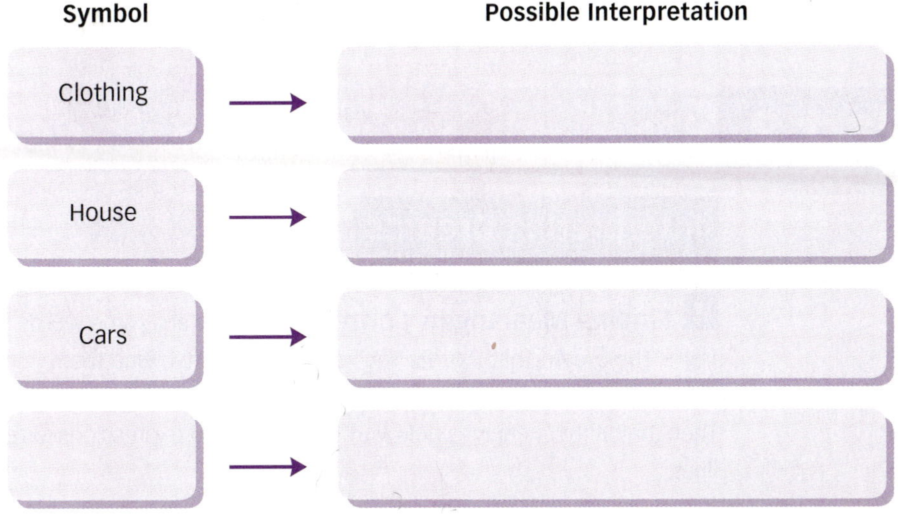

7 Freewriting Describe an interesting dream you've had, and try to explain why you had it. Write for 15 minutes without stopping.

8 Gathering Information Find information on an aspect of dreaming that interests you. Look for information in books, magazines, or online. Sample topics are:

- Psychological dream interpretation. For example, what might dreams say about your mental or emotional condition?
- Nonpsychological or folk interpretation of dreams. For example, do dreams predict the future or have some magical power?
- The importance of dreams in various cultures. For example, how do Native Americans, Senoi Malaysians, or people in your culture view dreams and dreaming?
- The physiological aspects of dreaming. For example, what happens to the body when you are dreaming?

Take notes on your article and prepare to present your research results to the class.

9 Sharing Results In small groups, present the information you gathered from your reading about dreams. In your presentation, include:

- An explanation of how you obtained your information
- A visual that relates to your topic (this can be a photo, sketch, or picture)
- At least one question that helps your classmates relate to your topic

Part 2 Focusing on Words and Phrases

Interpreting Dreams

1 Finding Meaning in Context Following are some words and expressions from "The Dream That Haunts You" on page 102–104. Find them in the passage. Notice their contexts—how they are used in a sentence—and try to guess their meanings. Then match the meanings below to the words and expressions. Write the letters on the lines.

Words and Expressions	Meanings
______ **1.** decipher (Line 89)	**a.** representation
______ **2.** exhilarating (Line 14)	**b.** not using the conscious mind
______ **3.** metaphors (Lines 42–43)	**c.** very upsetting
______ **4.** recur (Line 46)	**d.** the part of the mind that is not conscious
______ **5.** symbol (Line 43)	**e.** symbol
______ **6.** the unconscious (Lines 39–40)	**f.** decode; interpret
______ **7.** traumatic (Line 17)	**g.** very exciting
______ **8.** unconsciously (Line 45)	**h.** happen again

2 Using Expressions

Study these expressions for discussing dreams and dream interpretation. Find them in "The Dream That Haunts You" on pages 102–104 and notice how they are used in a sentence.

reflect [something]
symbolize [something or someone]
mark, stand for, indicate [something]
dream (of, about) [something or someone]
have a dream
indicate something (about) [something or someone]

Now complete each sentence with the correct form of one of the expressions. More than one expression may be correct in some sentences.

1. When Aaron ______________________ about flying, he realized he needed more freedom in his job.
2. In folklore, a dream about a missing tooth ______________________ losing a friend.
3. A dream about flying into an object may ______________________ feelings of being trapped in life.
4. A dream about flying might also ______________________ a desire to escape from something in your life.
5. When you dream about water, such as a tidal wave, it can ______________________ your feelings.
6. The ancients believed that dreams ______________________ visits from evil spirits.

3 **Using New Words and Expressions** Use the new words and expressions from this section to complete the following activities:

1. Choose one of the works of art from page 100, and write a paragraph interpreting the dream images. Use the words and expressions in this section.
2. Think again about the dream you described in your freewriting in Activity 7 on page 106. Write a paragraph interpreting the dream again, this time using the words and expressions in this section.
3. Choose one of the following dreams to interpret. Read the description, think about it, and then write an explanation of what you think it means.

   a. Boy, 5 years old: "I dreamed I was in the bathtub and the water began draining. My little sister went down the drain and just before she disappeared, she held her hand up. I caught it, and I pulled her out of the drain. I wasn't able to help our friend, Melanie, who went down the drain next. She didn't hold her hand up, so I couldn't save her."

   b. Woman, 35 years old: "A common dream I had as a child was running away from an erupting volcano. The hot lava was creeping faster and faster toward me. I ran as fast as I could to avoid being trapped and burned by the lava. I always woke up from this dream out of breath and scared!"

   c. Girl, 8 years old: "Last night I dreamed that a whole bunch of soldiers came into my bedroom through the window. There were carrying knives and guns and I was afraid they were going to kill me."

   d. Man, 50 years old: "I often dream that I've enrolled in a class and forget when it starts and where it's located. In the dream I'm wandering around campus looking for the correct building and feeling quite lost. I feel very guilty in this dream."

▲ A volcanic eruption

Part 3 Organizing and Developing Your Ideas

Paragraph Organization: Levels of Generality

Review Point

In a well-developed paragraph, the writer organizes his or her ideas in a logical order and explains how the supporting information is connected to the main idea.

New Points

An effective way to organize ideas in a paragraph is to use specific facts and illustrations to support general statements. Here are two ways to organize your ideas:

- Top-down organization
- Divided organization

Choose the pattern that best fits what you are writing about.

PARAGRAPH PATTERNS

Top-Down Organization

Look at the following example of **top-down** organization. It looks like a set of stairs: each idea in the paragraph moves one step down in generality.

1 Topic sentence (most general idea)
  2 More specific information about the topic
    3 More specific information about Sentence 2
      4 More specific information about Sentence 3
        5 More specific information about Sentence 4

Divided Organization

The following example, divided organization, looks like two sets of stairs, as the topic sentence of the paragraph has two parts.

1 Topic sentence (most general; may have two or more parts)
  2 First part (more specific)
    3 Fact or illustration related to the first part (very specific)
      4 More specific information about Sentence 3
  2 Second part (same level of specificity as the first part)
    3 Fact or illustration related to the second part (very specific)
      4 More specific information about Sentence 3

Organizing your ideas often begins at the brainstorming stage when you have a list of ideas on a topic. Before writing, note the general-to-specific relationships of the ideas in your notes.

1 Analyzing Divided Organization Look at the following example of some brainstorming notes and a divided organizational pattern. The notes are on the topic of anthropology as an academic field. Then answer the questions that follow.

Notes

Anthropology

The Great Apes

The Study of Primates
Cultural Anthropology
The Study of Linguistics
Physical Anthropology
Native American Languages

General-to-Specific Organization

1 *Anthropology*
  2 *Physical Anthropology*
    3 *The study of primates*
      4 *The great apes*
  2 *Cultural Anthropology*
    3 *The study of linguistics*
      4 *Native American languages*

1. What is the most general idea?

____

____

2. What two topics represent the next level of generality?

____

____

3. What are the relationships between the Level 3 ideas and the Level 2 ideas?

____

____

4. Why do "The great apes" and "Native American languages" appear where they do in this organizational pattern?

____

____

2 Practicing General-to-Specific Organization On page 111 is a list of ideas on the study of dreams. They are in no special order. Study the list, then organize the ideas in a general-to-specific pattern.

Notes

Dream interpretation: literal or symbolic

Example–dream of one's mother or friend

Dream of someone or something not found in one's day-to-day life–symbolic

Dream of someone or something in real life–literal

Example–dream of a dragon or some other fantastic animal

General-to-Specific Organization

1 ______________________________

  2 ______________________________

    3 ______________________________

  2 ______________________________

    3 ______________________________

3 Studying General-to-Specific Organization in a Paragraph Now, study this general-to-specific organization of ideas in the context of an entire paragraph. Read the following paragraph and answer the questions that follow.

▲ A dragon

(1) According to one author, dreams can have either a *literal* or a symbolic interpretation. (2) If a dream image represents someone the dreamer knows or an event that has actually occurred in the dreamer's life, then this image can be taken literally. (3) For example, if a person dreams of his or her mother, then most likely the dream is indeed about the person's mother, and the mother image should not be taken to represent anyone or anything else. (4) However, if a dream image does not represent a person or a thing that can be found in the dreamer's day-to-day existence, then the image can be taken as a symbol of something else. (5) For example, if a person dreams of a dragon or some other *exotic* animal he or she never comes in contact with, then the dreamer is free to interpret this image as a symbol of something else. (6) Therefore, when interpreting dreams, this author recommends looking for symbols only when a literal interpretation is impossible.

1. What is the topic of the first sentence? Is this idea general or specific?

___

___

2. What idea is expressed in Sentence 2? How does the idea in Sentence 2 relate to the idea of the first sentence?

___

___

3. What is the relationship, if any, of Sentence 4 to Sentence 2?

___

___

4. What is the relationship of Sentence 4 to the first sentence?

___

___

5. Explain the relationships of Sentences 3 and 5 to the rest of the paragraph.

___

___

6. What is the function of Sentence 6?

___

___

7. What organizational pattern would you use for this paragraph, top-down or divided?

___

___

Now diagram the ideas in the paragraph on page 111 on a separate piece of paper. (Hint: Sentence 6, the conclusion, has the same level of generality as Sentence 1.)

Focus on Testing

"Drawing" Your Ideas for TOEFL® iBT Writing

In several parts of this chapter, you have read about organizational patterns that can be shown in a diagram. Using lines, drawing a sketch, or making a diagram or chart is often a helpful way to plan idea relationships to make in your response to a writing task on the Internet-based TOEFL® iBT.

The difficulty is that you have very little time to complete either of the two tasks on the TOEFL® iBT—30 minutes for the independent response, 20 minutes for the integrated response. Within these time limits, you must complete all stages of your writing process: planning, writing, and revising. There is not much time for careful planning.

Practice: Look again at the first reading in this chapter, "The Dream that Haunts You." Imagine that you must respond to the prompt below. Set a timer for five minutes. During that time, create an organizer to lay out your ideas for a response. You may choose any type of organizer that you think will work best for you. After you have finished, do the exercise again with another type of organizer. Then compare your organizers to those done by one or two other students.

Prompt: Although some researchers say dreams are nonsense (meaningless), others think dreams do have meaning. Using information from the reading, explain what kinds of meaning dreams might have, according to researchers.

4 Analyzing Levels of Generality

Read the paragraph below and study the relationships between ideas in the sentences. Number each sentence according to its level of generality. The most general ideas will be numbered 1, and the most specific ideas will be 3.

( ) In the last several decades, researchers have learned a great deal about the frequency and duration of dreams, which can be observed in two ways.

( ) One way is to connect wires from an amplifying and recording device, called an electroencephalograph, to the sleeper's head. ( ) This instrument registers "brain waves," which are tiny changes in the electrical potential of the brain at rest. ( ) A certain pattern of these brain waves indicates dreaming. ( ) Another way scientists collect data on dreams is by observing the sleeper's eyes. ( ) There is active eye movement when a person dreams. ( ) This eye movement can be seen through closed eyelids and recorded automatically on moving paper tape. ( ) From these two methods, scientists have found that everyone dreams four to six times a night and that each dream lasts between 15 and 20 minutes. ( ) If you don't think you dream, you simply don't remember your dreams!

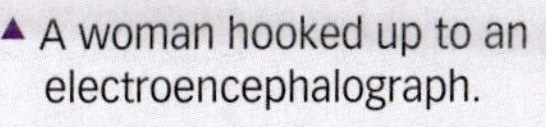

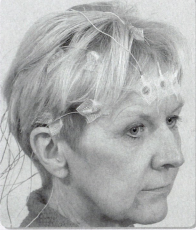

▲ A woman hooked up to an electroencephalograph.

5 Practicing Top-down Organization Write two paragraphs on a folk belief or saying about dreams from your country or another country. For the first paragraph, use the top-down organizational pattern:

1
  2
    3
      4
        5
          6 (optional)
Conclusion

Note that you will be giving increasingly specific information about your main idea as you proceed. Your paragraph will have five or six sentences. Make sure that you include all the levels of generality shown in the preceding diagram. Then rewrite the paragraph using this divided organizational pattern:

1
  2
    3
      4
  2
    3
      4
Conclusion

Note that in this paragraph you will be giving increasingly specific information about two aspects of your main idea. This paragraph will be at least eight sentences long. Make sure that you include all the levels of generality shown in the outline above.

6 Practicing What You've Learned Choose a paragraph from the body of one of your previous essays. Reread it and see how well it is organized. Try to diagram it as you did the preceding paragraph. If you cannot diagram it, rewrite it, paying attention to its organizational pattern.

Writing Product

7 Writing about a Dream Write an essay on the following topic using the ideas that you've discussed and written about so far in this chapter.

> Write about a dream you've had, a dream that someone told you about, or a dream that you read about. First, describe the dream. Then, write about one or more possible interpretations.

▲ A memory of a dream

Part 4 Evaluating Your Writing

Use the following rubric to score your writing. Read the rubric with your class, then give your writing a score. A classmate and a teacher will score your writing also and explain reasons for their scores. If you want to revise and improve this essay or writing from a previous chapter, you can do it now.

Rubric for Writing About a Dream

Score	Description
3 **Excellent**	▪ **Content:** Writing presents a dream and provides one or more reasonable interpretations through reference to symbols, examples, experiences, and/or background information. ▪ **Organization:** Ideas are organized to support and explain main idea through an introduction, a main idea, body paragraphs, and a conclusion; ideas follow a logical sequence and are easy to follow. ▪ **Vocabulary and Sentence Structure:** Vocabulary is specific and descriptive; sentence types are varied. ▪ **Grammar:** Subjects and verbs agree; common grammar problems (pronouns, articles, and plurals) are minimal so that meaning is clear. ▪ **Spelling and Mechanics:** Most words are spelled correctly, and punctuation is correct.
2 **Adequate**	▪ **Content:** Writing presents a dream and interprets it, although reader may have questions. ▪ **Organization:** Ideas are organized and there is a clear beginning, middle, and end; main idea is clear; some parts may be undeveloped. ▪ **Vocabulary and Sentence Structure:** Vocabulary is descriptive; sentences are mostly the same type. ▪ **Grammar:** Subjects and verbs mostly agree; common grammar problems (pronouns, articles, and plurals) are distracting. ▪ **Spelling and Mechanics:** Some distracting spelling and/or punctuation mistakes.

1 **Developing**	▪ **Content:** Writing does not present a dream clearly or interpret it sufficiently. ▪ **Organization:** Ideas do not follow essay format and are confusing or too brief. ▪ **Vocabulary and Sentence Structure:** Vocabulary is limited and/or there are too many mistakes to understand and/or follow the ideas; sentences have mistakes. ▪ **Grammar:** Many common grammar problems (pronouns, articles, and plurals) that are confusing to the reader. ▪ **Spelling and Mechanics:** Many distracting spelling and/or punctuation mistakes.

Self-Assessment Log

In this chapter, you worked through the following activities. How much did each of them help you become a better writer? Check *A lot*, *A little*, or *Not at all*.

	A lot	**A little**	**Not at all**
I discussed art that deals with dreams.	❑	❑	❑
I read about the meaning of dreams.	❑	❑	❑
I learned how to interpret symbols.	❑	❑	❑
I gathered and shared information about dreams.	❑	❑	❑
I learned and used vocabulary for writing about dreams.	❑	❑	❑
I organized paragraphs according to levels of generality.	❑	❑	❑
I evaluated my essay.	❑	❑	❑
(Add something) ________________________________	❑	❑	❑

____

Chapter 7

Working

In This Chapter

Genre Focus: Analysis

Writing Product

In this chapter, you'll write about success at work.

Writing Process

- Discuss business success in different cultures.
- Read about different business styles.
- Make inferences.
- Interview a businessperson.
- Learn and use vocabulary for writing about work.
- Describe causes and effects.

"What I know is, that if you do work that you love, and the work fulfills you, the rest will come."

—Oprah Winfrey
American talk show host, actress, and entrepreneur (1954–)

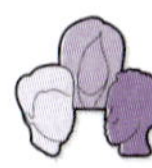

Connecting to the Topic

1. What is the secret to success in business?
2. Would you like a career in business?
3. In what type of job would you be most successful?

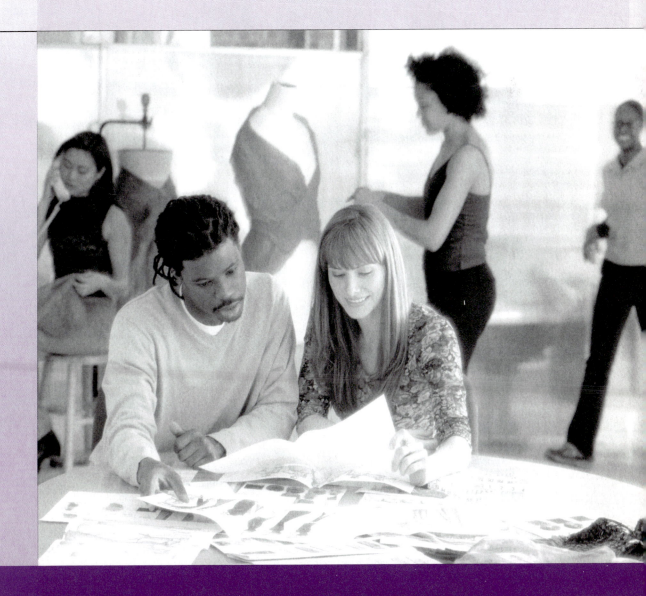

Part 1 Preparing to Write

Getting Started

1 Discussing Work Think about what it might be like to work with people from different cultures. Study the pictures below and answer the questions that follow.

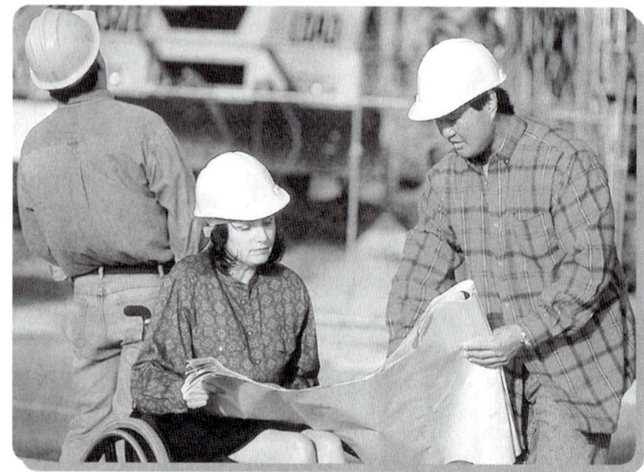

▲ Designing a resort in Abu Dhabi

▲ Giving a presentation in Korea

▲ Negotiating a contract in Japan

▲ Growing plants for export in Brazil

1. In each situation shown in the photos what might a businessperson have to know about the country or culture in order to be successful?

____

____

____

____

2. What communication problems do you think might occur in these situations?

____

____

____

____

2 Taking a Quiz Ideas about business vary from culture to culture. Are your ideas different from those of your classmates? Take the following quiz to find out. Read each sentence. Circle A if you agree with it and D if you disagree with it. Then compare your answers with those of your classmates. Discuss if your opinions are personal or cultural.

1. A D When a company hires a new employee, it should take into consideration the personal relationships the candidate is likely to form with others in the company; this is more important than job qualifications.
2. A D Time equals money; it's important to get things done quickly.
3. A D Teamwork is very important.
4. A D Employees should discuss their problems with their supervisors frequently.
5. A D Personal relationships are very important in any business transaction.
6. A D Written contracts and agreements are not necessary; a person's word is enough in making a business deal.
7. A D Individual employees are responsible for the success of their company as a whole, not just for their own work.
8. A D Employees should always show respect when they talk to people in higher positions.
9. A D A person's sex or race should not influence whether or not a company hires him or her.
10. A D Only the manager should make decisions that affect his or her employees, not the employees themselves.

3 Preparing to Read Below is an excerpt from a book about doing business in Japan. In this excerpt, the author describes a Japanese decision-making style: decision making by consensus (group decision making). Before you read, answer these questions.

1. How do you make an important decision?

____

____

____

2. How do you think people make decisions at work? As a group? Or does one person make the decision? Does decision making take a long time? Why or why not? Is making decisions at work different from making personal decisions?

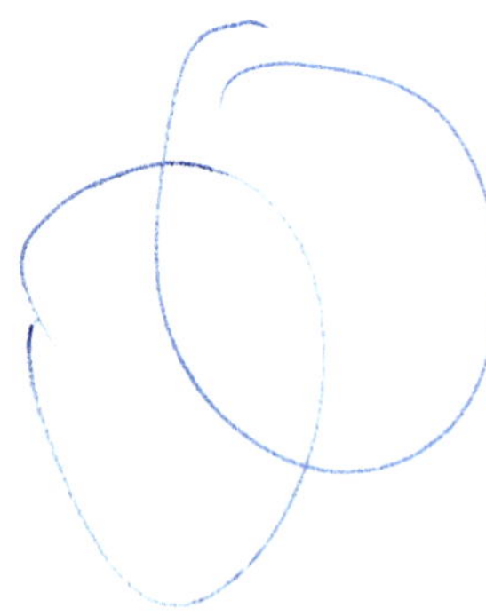

____

____

____

3. How might culture affect decision making? What might contribute to successful decision making in a crosscultural work situation?

____

____

____

Decision by Consensus

A One of the most important differences in management style between Japanese management and that in most other countries lies in the area of decision making. Westerners often find the Japanese method of making decisions to be extremely slow. However, most people do not realize the different thought processes and procedures that are going on during Japanese-style decision making.

B Westerners tend to make major decisions at the top, in board meetings, among department heads (high-level managers). They then "pass the word" down to lower-level managers and others to implement and carry out the decision. The Japanese do the opposite. Their system, commonly known as *ringi*, is the corporate version of "government by consensus."

C With *ringi*, decisions are not made "on high" and given to lower-level employees to be implemented. Rather, they are proposed from below and move upward. In this process, the decision receives additional input and approvals after much discussion through all levels of the company.

D "One should think of the system as a filter through which ideas pass," says Robert T. Moran. "The whole process, as it slowly goes through various levels of the company, can last from two to three weeks to a matter of months. Each level takes its own time to consider the details. If the matter is complex or sensitive, it can take even longer."

E For decisions that are not of really major importance, approvals can be given by various individuals (or by groups). But when any decision is of great importance, the Japanese look for broad consensus. *Ringi* should be seen as a "process" rather than a system. It gives management the choice of a broad selection of practical choices. Often, the person who initiates an idea is a section chief. He proposes an idea (which may have been suggested to him by one of his workers). He gets his section members to research it; they all discuss it. When satisfied, he passes it up to the higher levels of management.

F Even junior members take part in all this deliberation. It is considered part of their training. It is also a way to develop company motivation. The idea is considered all the way up until it reaches the president. If he approves it, it will have been seen and considered by almost everyone who could be in any way involved in the final implementation. One can imagine the bargaining, persuasion, trading of favors, seeking of support, and general "lobbying" that goes on throughout the process! All of this is known as *nemawashi*, which means "binding up the roots." (This suggests the image of a tree that will survive only if everything is properly prepared in advance.)

G One of the major benefits of *ringi* is that it avoids the possibility of any one person being "personally responsible" for a decision. When responsibility is spread out to many people, no one "loses face" (is embarrassed).

H "Sometimes the delays in making even simple decisions are almost unbearable," said a fast-moving American executive who works with a worldwide hotel chain. "Everybody has to be involved with everything," he continued. "It takes forever. As far as I am concerned, this is without a doubt the very hardest part of working for a Japanese company. You feel as if you can never get a decision on anything, large or small."

I "By the time the decision is finally made," added another, "I have usually lost interest in it and am involved in something else."

J If you try to hurry the process, it does more harm than good. The Japanese do not like pressure. Obviously, frustrated Westerners will be itching to know what is going on as the silence continues for weeks or months. You submit a proposal or an inquiry. Nothing happens. Who is holding it up?

What is happening? Did the message ever get through?

K If the decision that you are waiting for relates to a new idea, perhaps something you have initiated, then you can count on a really long delay. If, on the other hand, the company is merely talking about changes to an idea that they have already agreed to, then it may take considerably less time for a reply.

L But you will rarely get quick action unless, as one experienced businessperson said, "You have gold that is $7.00 on the open market and are willing to sell it for $6.00. Then you will get action without delay." You may occasionally meet Japanese who will try to shorten the normal time in consideration of Western impatience. But don't expect it.

M In writing this book, I asked several businesspeople who work well with the Japanese what they think is the single biggest factor in their success. In every single case the first quality that they mentioned was "patience, patience, and still more patience." They all agreed: "If you lose your patience or get upset, you are likely to leave without accomplishing anything."

N Although the *ringi* system is slow, no one can complain afterwards. The result is harmonious feelings and bad feelings are lessened—if not eliminated, because when the process has reached a certain stage, no one feels he can "buck the tide." So, he goes along with it. After that, he is effectively silenced. Direct opposition is rarely effective among the Japanese. One achieves more by the persuading and negotiating—one might say "lobbying"—that is allowed through *nemawashi*.

O Actually, the delay that happens before a decision is made may not be as great as it sometimes appears when compared with Western systems. Where the Western "top-down" approach to decision making is used, the original plan or agreement is frequently made relatively quickly at the top in the boardroom. However, delays of weeks or months may follow while lower-level employees first learn about the decision and are then persuaded to support it. Both steps are necessary before a plan can actually be implemented. When lower-level employees have not participated in making the decision, misunderstandings, disagreement, or other delays frequently occur.

P In Japan, in contrast, once the decision is finally made, all relevant staff members understand it thoroughly. They are familiar with it because they were involved with it in the early stages. So, although it may take a long time to arrive at the decision, once approval has been given, they can implement it rapidly and smoothly. The final time difference between the two systems, therefore, may not be as far apart as it can sometimes seem.

Q Furthermore, in the Japanese system, people in lower-level positions feel they have been involved. They have been able—often urged—to suggest proposals, projects, or refinements. Japanese bosses believe in encouraging suggestions from the lower-level employees. The idea of creating a consensus that incorporates everyone in the organization is at the heart of Japanese business philosophy and methods. 99

—Alison Lanier, *The Rising Sun on Main Street: Working with the Japanese.*

4 Understanding the Reading First, answer the following questions:

1. What are the main differences between the Western decison-making process and that of the Japanese? Complete the following graphic organizer to list the differences and give examples.

Western Decision Making	Japanese Decision Making
1. Top-down	1. down – Top
Example: Heads to employees	Example: employees to heads
2. fast	2. Takes a lot of time
Example: Takes short time.	Example: Slow
3. High level of managers	3. Many people invloved
Example: discussion between heads (high level)	Example: everyone in company involved.

2. Pretend that you are a Japanese businessperson. You are doing business in the United States with an American company. The company is in the process of making an important decision that will affect you. How would you describe the American decision-making process?

Even though I didn't know about it, I didn't discuss about it. I have to follow the rule that what the heads said.

3. Do you or does anyone in your class have experience with Japanese business? If so, answer the following question: Do you think that the author of the article has presented a correct picture of the Japanese decision-making process?

4. Now form small groups. Practice making a decision by consensus. Make a decision about one of the following topics. Create a consensus; that is, make sure everyone in the group is involved. Then, if possible, implement your decision. Afterward, discuss how you felt about the consensus process.

- Decide on a new seating arrangement in your class.
- Decide on a freewriting topic for this chapter.
- Decide if and/or when to take a break during class.
- Decide if and/or when to have a class party.
- Your topic: ______________________________

Strategy

Thinking Critically: *Making Inferences*

Making an inference about what you read means understanding information that is not directly stated. The inference is a kind of guess, but the guess is based on information in the reading material. Making inferences is a useful academic thinking skill.

5 Practicing Making Inferences The author of "Decision by Consensus" discusses the advantages and disadvantages of the Japanese decision-making process. Her point of view is American. Although she doesn't directly discuss the advantages and disadvantages of the American decision-making process, based on other material in the excerpt, you can infer what they are. Summarize the two systems in the following graphic organizer. You will have to infer the American advantages and disadvantages based on the material in the excerpt.

	Ringi	American Decision-Making Process
Advantages		
Disadvantages		

6 Freewriting If you decided on a Freewriting topic in item 4 above, write about that topic for 20 minutes without stopping. If you didn't, write for 20 minutes without stopping on your ideas about how to be successful at work, either in your own culture or in another culture.

7 Gathering Information Conduct an interview in which you ask a business-person to describe his or her work environment. Include questions such as the following, as well as some of your own:

- Where do you work? What kind of company is it?
- What is your job?
- What's it like to work there? Describe the setting. What is the equipment like?
- How are the relationships among the employees?
- What management styles are used? How do managers inspire employees? Do lower-level employees participate in decison making?
- What do you like about your job? What don't you like about your job?
- Do you feel successful?
- In your opinion, what is the most important quality that contributes to success at work?
- Your questions: ______________________________

8 Sharing Results Present the results of your interview to the class. Organize your presentation around the answer to the following question: What qualities, policies, or practices ensure success at work?

Part 2 Focusing on Words and Phrases

Describing Work in a Multicultural Setting

1 Finding Meaning in Context Below are some words and expressions from "Decision by Consensus" on pages 122–125. Find them in the passage. Notice their contexts—how they are used in a sentence—and try to guess their meanings. Then match the meanings below to the words and expressions. Write the letters on the lines.

Words and Expressions	Meanings
_____ **1.** carry out (Line 9)	**a.** how decisions are made and implemented
_____ **2.** deliberation (Line 30)	**b.** tell others
_____ **3.** harmonious (Line 71)	**c.** accomplish
_____ **4.** initiated (Line 56)	**d.** at the upper levels
_____ **5.** lessened (Line 71)	**e.** discussion
_____ **6.** lobbying (Lines 76–77)	**f.** persuading
_____ **7.** management style (Line 1)	**g.** started
_____ **8.** on high (Line 12)	**h.** in agreement
_____ **9.** pass the word (Line 8)	**i.** made smaller or less important
_____ **10.** refinements (Line 96)	**j.** improvements

EXPRESSIONS FOR INTRODUCING CAUSE AND EFFECT

Study these expressions for introducing causes and effects.
(Note: A = cause, B = effect).

Expressions	Examples
B *results from* A.	Harmony results from the practice of *ringi.*
A *results in* B.	The *ringi* system results in harmony.
A *causes* B.	The *ringi* system causes harmony.
B *is the result of* A.	Harmony is the result of the *ringi* system.
Because of A, B.	Because of *ringi,* power struggles are minimized.

2 Using Expressions

Find the expressions above in "Decision by Consensus" on pages 122–125 and notice how they are used in a sentence.

Now complete each sentence below with the correct form of one of the expressions. More than one expression may be correct in some sentences.

1. Many people who were interviewed said that their success at work ______________ hard work.
2. Chris feels that her new job ______________ important contacts that she had in the company.
3. ______________ his degree in business, Jack is having an easy time getting job interviews.
4. Good communications skills ______________ good relationships at work.
5. A lack of communication often ______________ disharmony at work.
6. Often, success at work ______________ making a wise career choice.

3 Using New Words and Expressions

Use the new words and expressions from this section to complete the following activities:

1. Write a paragraph based on your topic for your freewriting in Activity 6 on page 126.
2. Write one or more paragraphs about your interview in Activity 7 on page 127.
3. Write a paragraph about the causes or effects of a cultural misunderstanding in a business or educational situation.

Part 3 Organizing and Developing Your Ideas

Cause and Effect

Review Point

- The organizational pattern you choose for an essay depends on the topic of the essay.

New Points

- One way to make a point in an essay is to show a causal relationship.
- You can describe a causal relationship in a sentence, a paragraph, or an entire essay.
- There are two kinds of causal relationships: a simple one, where one action leads to another (a → b), and a complex one, where one cause leads to a result, which then leads to another result (a → b → c). This is called a *causal chain*.

▲ Businesspeople in the U.S. conducting a video conference with a client in Japan

CAUSAL RELATIONSHIPS

Sentence 1: The rise in global business has increased (a) → the need to understand cultural interactions within organizations. (b)

Sentence 2: A lack of knowledge about cross-cultural negotiations (a)
can lead to → misunderstanding in a business transaction (b)
that can result in → loss of profits in the long run. (c)

1 Analyzing Causes and Effects Look at these examples of the two types of causal relationships. Both sentences 1 and 2 above describe causes and effects. Which words or expressions indicate causes and which words or expressions indicate effects? Make a list:

Causes	Effects

2 Using Graphic Organizers A causal chain can be as long as necessary to cover all the important causes and effects of your subject. Complete the following graphic organizers by adding the missing information. Use your imagination.

1.
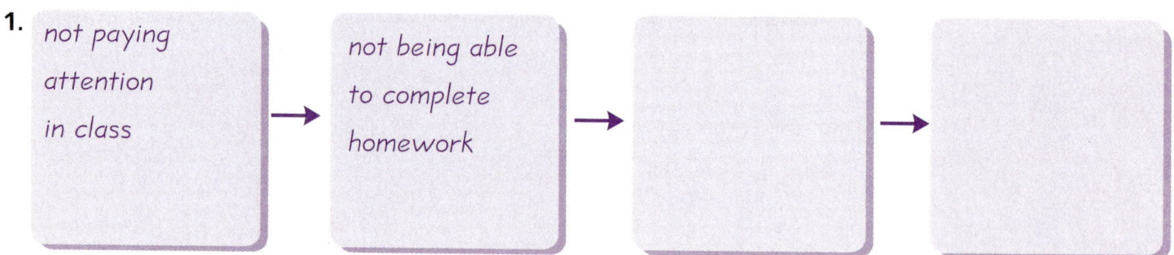

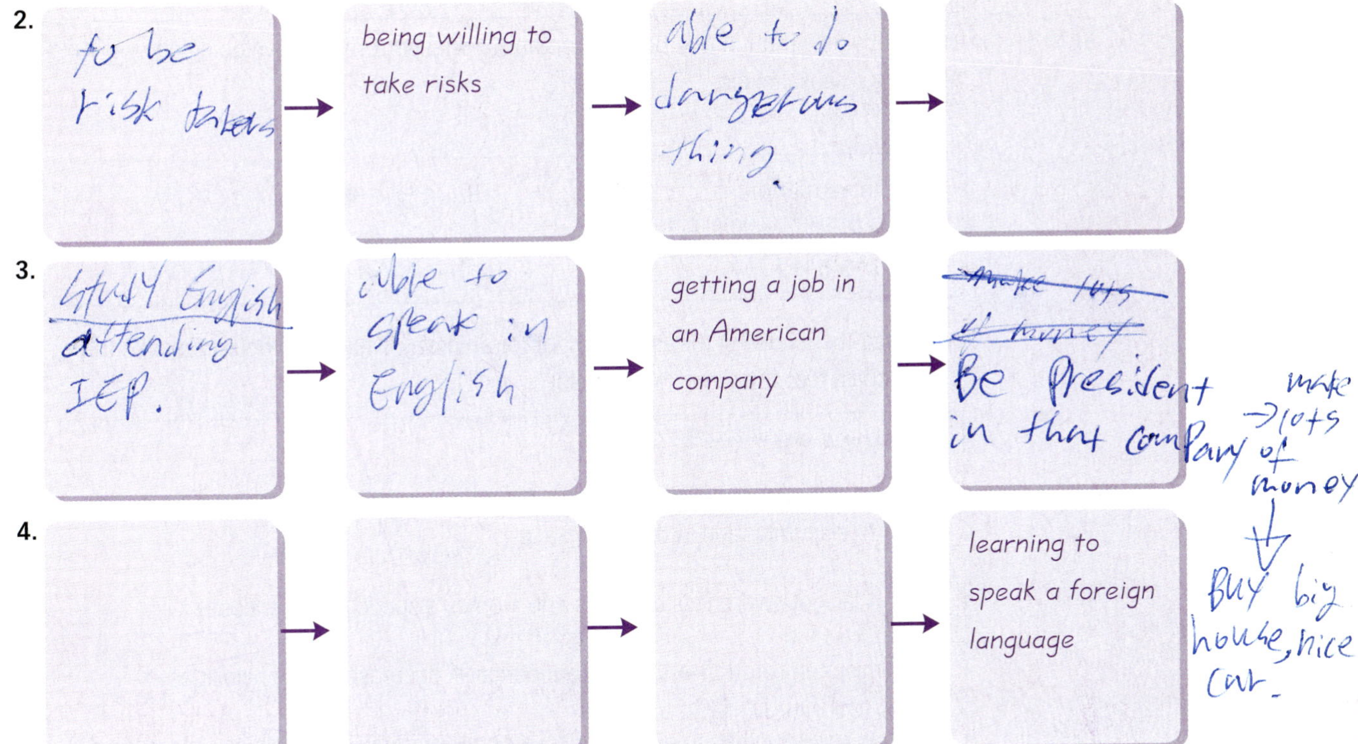

Causal Chain Essay Organization I

New Points

- The thesis statement of a causal chain essay presents the initial cause and final result; the body paragraphs explain the process from cause to result in detail.
- There are many ways to organize a causal chain; however, in order for the chain to be the subject of an entire essay, there must be enough intermediate steps to make up more than one body paragraph.
- Another way to organize a causal chain essay is to begin with the final result and work backward to the initial cause.

Look at this diagram of one possible organizational pattern for developing an essay showing a causal chain:

I. Introduction
Thesis Statement: a–f

II. a → b → c

III. d → e → f

IV. Conclusion

Now read the following thesis statement for an essay. Then read the six steps in the causal chain that the writer will develop.

a → b → c → d → e → f

A lack of awareness of the differences between men's and women's speech can lead to discrimination in the workplace.

(a) A lack of awareness of men's and women's speech differences → (b) misinterpretation → (c) lack of confidence → (d) decreased responsibilities → (e) no opportunities to exhibit skills → (f) no promotion (which is discriminatory)

Causal Chain Essay Organization II

Read the following example of a thesis statement for this type of essay organization:

John ended up resigning from his position in the company and returning to the United States as a result of his lack of knowledge of Japanese business styles.

3 Writing a Causal Chain Based on what you've learned about Japanese and Western business styles in this chapter, write causes that could be included as intermediate steps in the development of this essay

John's lack of knowledge about Japanese business styles →

____ →

____ →

____ →

____ →

John resigned from his job.

TOEFL® IBT

Focus on Testing

Having a Repertoire of Organizational Patterns

Part 3 presents two ways of organizing a cause-and-effect essay. Knowing two or three organizational patterns for a particular essay type will help you plan and write essays faster in test-taking situations.

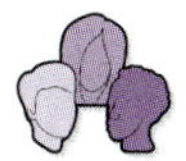

4 Developing a Causal Chain Work in amall groups. Begin with the single cause provided below, and take it as far as possible by having individual students take turns giving direct and logical results that then lead to further results. How long can you make your causal chain?

Initial cause: Traveling to another country → ____________________

→ ____________________ → ____________________ → ____________________

→ ____________________ → ____________________ → and so on.

5 Writing a Causal Chain Thesis Statement Write a thesis statement for a causal-chain essay based on "Decision by Consensus" on pages 122–125.

____

____

____

6 Practicing What You've Learned Rewrite the revision of your freewriting that you did in Activity 3 on page 128. This time, show a causal relationship.

Writing Product

7 Writing About Success at Work Write an essay on the following topic, using the ideas that you've discussed and written about so far in this chapter.

What important quality contributes to success at work?

Part 4 Evaluating for Rewriting

Use the following rubric to score your writing. Read the rubric with your class, then give your writing a score. A classmate and a teacher will score your writing also and explain reasons for their scores. If you want to revise and improve this essay or an essay or other writing from a previous chapter, you can do it now.

Rubric for Writing About Qualities That Contribute to Success at Work

Score	Description
3 **Excellent**	▪ **Content:** Writing presents one or more qualities that contribute to success at work; ideas are supported through examples, experiences, facts, and/or background statistics. ▪ **Organization:** Ideas are organized to support and explain main idea through an introduction, a main idea, body paragraphs, and a conclusion; ideas follow a logical sequence and are easy to follow. ▪ **Vocabulary and Sentence Structure:** Vocabulary is specific and descriptive; sentence types are varied. ▪ **Grammar:** Subjects and verbs agree; common grammar problems (pronouns, articles, and plurals) are minimal so that meaning is clear. ▪ **Spelling and Mechanics:** Most words are spelled correctly and punctuation is correct.
2 **Adequate**	▪ **Content:** Writing presents a quality that contributes to success at work; writing includes reasons and examples. ▪ **Organization:** Ideas are organized and there is a clear beginning, middle, and end; main idea is clear; some parts may be undeveloped. ▪ **Vocabulary and Sentence Structure:** Vocabulary is descriptive; sentences are mostly the same type. ▪ **Grammar:** Subjects and verbs mostly agree; common grammar problems (pronouns, articles, and plurals) are distracting. ▪ **Spelling and Mechanics:** There are some distracting spelling and/or punctuation mistakes.

1 **Developing**	■ **Content:** Writing does not clearly present a quality that contributes to success at work; writing does not include convincing or sufficient reasons and/or examples. ■ **Organization:** Ideas do not follow essay format and are confusing or too brief. ■ **Vocabulary and Sentence Structure:** Vocabulary is limited and/or there are too many mistakes to understand and/or follow the ideas; sentences have mistakes. ■ **Grammar:** Many common grammar problems (pronouns, articles, and plurals) are confusing to the reader. ■ **Spelling and Mechanics:** There are many distracting spelling and/or punctuation mistakes.

Self-Assessment Log

In this chapter, you worked through the following activities. How much did each of them help you become a better writer? Check *A lot, A little,* or *Not at all.*

	A lot	**A little**	**Not at all**
I discussed business success in different cultures.	❑	❑	❑
I read about different business styles.	❑	❑	❑
I practiced making inferences.	❑	❑	❑
I interviewed a businessperson.	❑	❑	❑
I learned and used vocabulary for writing about work.	❑	❑	❑
I used a simple cause and effect organizational pattern in my essay.	❑	❑	❑
I used a causal chain organizational pattern in my essay.	❑	❑	❑
I evaluated my essay.	❑	❑	❑
(Add something) ________________________________	❑	❑	❑

____

Chapter 8

Breakthroughs

In This Chapter

Genre Focus: Definition

Writing Product

In this chapter, you'll write about a development in energy conservation.

Writing Process

- Discuss solar-powered devices.
- Read about an innovation in solar power.
- Expand on the literal meaning of words.
- Gather and share information about energy technology.
- Learn and use vocabulary for describing energy and technology.
- Describe processes.

"The best way to predict the future is to invent it."

—Alan Kay
(American pioneer of personal computing, 1940–)

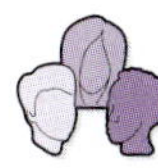

Connecting to the Topic

1. What are some different types of energy sources?
2. What are the advantages and disadvantages of various types of energy sources?
3. What new kinds of energy sources might there be in the future?

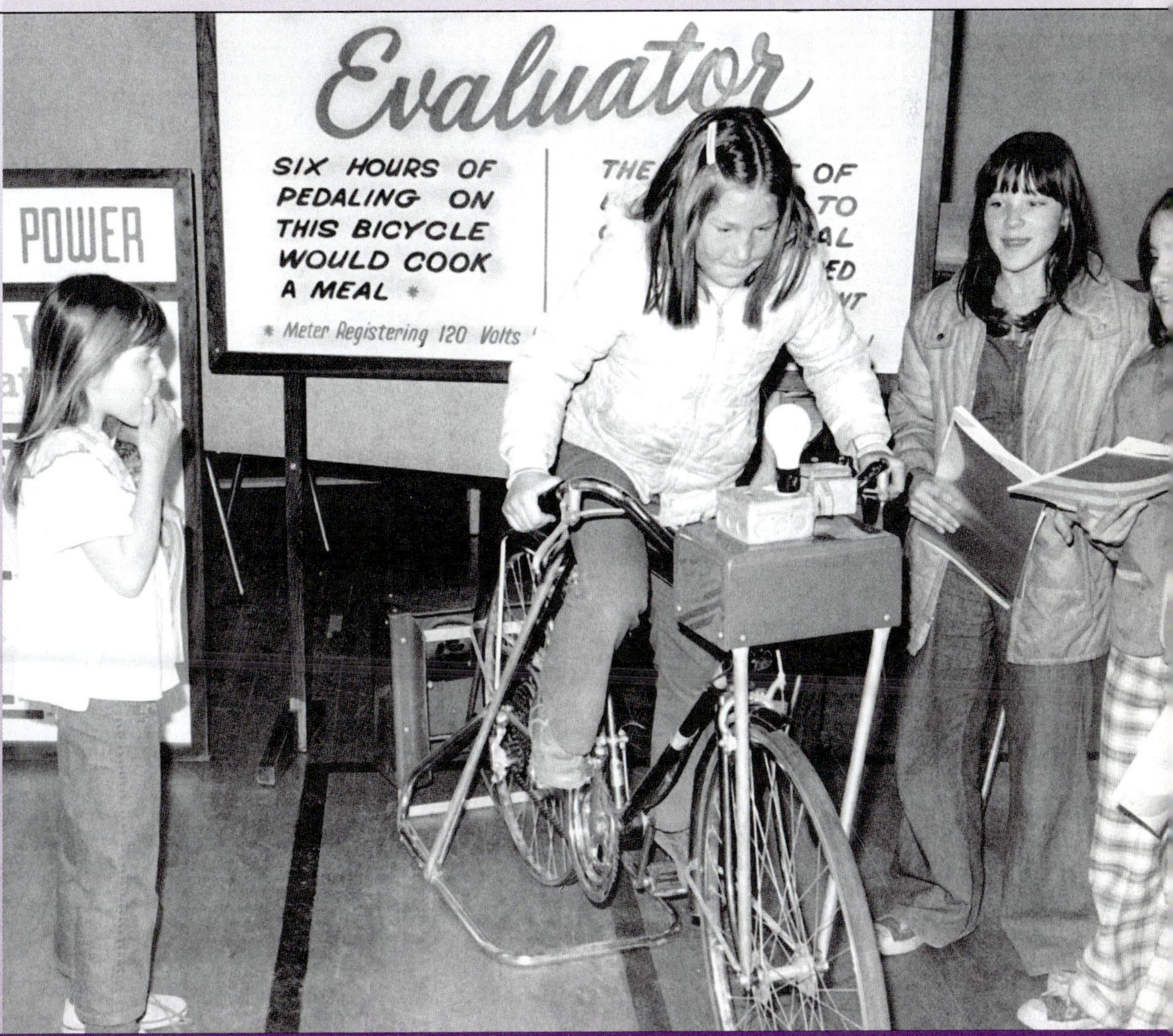

Part 1 Preparing To Write

Getting Started

1 Discussing Solar Power Look at these photos that show current applications of solar power, then discuss the questions that follow.

▲ Solar panels heat and provide electricity for this building.

▲ Folding solar panel provides power for his laptop computer.

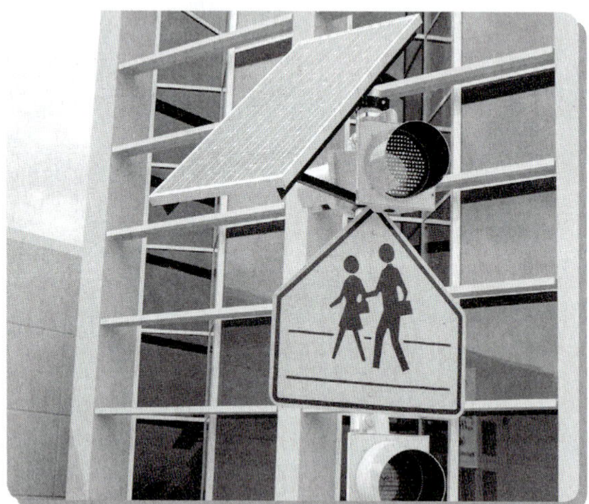

▲ Solar-powered street sign and lights can save cities money.

▲ Solar-powered toys are fun and energy-efficient.

1. Which of these solar-powered devices have you seen or used?

____

____

2. What are some other applications of solar power?

____

____

3. What are some of the conditions that must exist for solar power to work?

____

____

4. Can you explain how solar power works? If so, try to give a brief explanation to your group members.

____

____

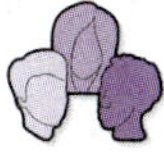

2 Discussing Advantages and Disadvantages Discuss the advantages and disadvantages of some other energy sources. Think about the following questions. Which energy sources:

- are expensive?
- are efficient?
- are difficult to build?
- require special weather conditions?
- require special equipment?

What are the potential hazards of each energy source? Record your answers in this graphic organizer.

Energy Source	Advantages	Disadvantages
1. wind		
2. sun		
3. oil		

Energy Source	Advantages	Disadvantages
4. coal		
5. nuclear power		
6. hydroelectric power		

3 Preparing to Read You are going to read an article about a breakthrough in solar power. Before you read, answer the following questions.

1. The technology that you are going to read about uses plastic. Describe the qualities of plastic. That is, what adjectives can you use to describe it? Where does it come from? Is it expensive? What forms does it have? (Think about plastic products around your home.)

2. What do you know about *nanotechnology?* (Hint: Nano is Greek for "small.") If you know anything about nanotechnology, describe some of its applications.

3. The sun radiates light to the Earth. Can we see all of it? What do you call the sun rays that we cannot see?

Spray-On Solar-Power Cells Are True Breakthrough

A Scientists have invented a plastic solar cell that can turn the sun's power into electrical energy, even on a cloudy day.

B The plastic material uses nanotechnology and contains the first solar cells able to harness the sun's invisible, infrared rays. The breakthrough has led theorists to predict that plastic solar cells could one day become five times more efficient than current solar cell technology.

C Like paint, the material can be sprayed onto other materials and used as portable electricity. A sweater coated in the material could power a cell phone or other wireless devices. A hydrogen-powered car painted with the film could potentially convert enough energy into electricity to continually recharge the car's battery.

D The researchers envision that one day "solar farms" consisting of the plastic material could be rolled across deserts to generate enough clean energy to supply the entire planet's power needs.

E "The sunlight that reaches the Earth's surface delivers 10,000 times more energy than we use," said Ted Sargent, an electrical and computer engineering professor at the University of Toronto. Sargent is one of the inventors of the new plastic material.

F "If we could cover 0.1 percent of the Earth's surface with large-area solar cells," he said, "we could in principle replace all of our energy habits with a source of power which is clean and renewable."

Infrared Power

G Plastic solar cells are not new. But existing materials are only able to harness the sun's visible light. While half of the sun's power lies in the visible spectrum, the other half lies in the infrared spectrum.

H The new material is the first plastic composite that is able to harness the infrared part of the spectrum.

I "Everything that's warm gives off some heat. Even people and animals give off heat," Sargent said. "So there actually is some power remaining in the infrared spectrum, even when it appears to us to be dark outside."

J The researchers combined specially designed nano particles called quantum dots with a polymer to make the plastic that can detect energy in the infrared.

K With further advances, the new plastic "could allow up to 30 percent of the sun's radiant energy to be harnessed, compared to 6 percent in today's best plastic solar cells," said Peter Peumans, a Stanford University electrical engineering professor who studied the work.

Electrical Sweaters

L The new material could make technology truly wireless.

M "We have this expectation that we don't have to plug into a phone jack anymore to talk on the phone, but we're resigned to the fact that we have to plug into an electrical outlet to recharge the batteries," Sargent said. In other words, we have wireless communication, but not wireless power.

N He said the plastic coating could be woven into a shirt or sweater and used to charge an item like a cell phone.

O "A sweater is already absorbing all sorts of light, both in the infrared and the visible," said Sargent. "Instead of just turning that into heat, as it currently does, imagine if it were to turn that into electricity."

P Other possibilities include energy-saving plastic sheeting that could be placed onto a rooftop to supply heating needs, or solar cell window coating that could let in enough infrared light to power home appliances.

Q *Cost-Effectiveness*

Ultimately, a large amount of the sun's energy could be harnessed through "solar farms" and used to power all our energy needs, the researchers predict.

R "This could potentially displace other sources of electrical production that produce greenhouse gases, such as coal," Sargent said.

In Japan, the world's largest solar-power market, the government expects that 50 percent of residential power supply will come from solar power by 2030, up from a fraction of a percent today.

S The biggest obstacle facing solar power is cost-effectiveness. At a current cost of 25 to 50 cents per kilowatt-hour, solar power is significantly more expensive than conventional electrical power for residences. Average U.S. residential power prices are less than ten cents per kilowatt-hour, according to experts.

T But that could change. Energy-saving plastic sheeting has the potential to turn the sun's power into a clean, green, convenient source of energy.

—Adapted from Stefan Lovren, "Spray-On Solar-Power Cells Are True Breakthrough"

4 Understanding the Reading In small groups, discuss the answers to the following questions.

1. What are sprayable solar power cells? Why are they innovative? That is, how are they different from plastic solar cells that already exist?

____

____

2. What are some of the uses of this new technology?

____

____

3. How much of the sun's energy is used by current solar-power technology? How much could be used if this new technology is developed further?

____

____

4. What are some of the advantages of this new solar technology?

____

____

5. What country might benefit the most from the new technology?

____

____

Strategy

Thinking Critically: *Expanding on the Literal Meanings of Words*

Words often have more than one meaning. You can use context to help you understand how familiar words take on new meanings. This is an important critical thinking skill.

5 Practicing Finding New Word Meanings Below are some words from the article you just read. Read the most common meaning of each word, then try to guess the secondary meaning used in the article.

1. The new material is the first plastic composite that is able to harness the infrared part of the spectrum.
   Definition 1: **harness** *(noun):* A system of straps, buckles, chains, and hooks attached to an animal to enable it to pull a load.

   Definition 2: ____

2. The researchers envision that one day "solar farms" consisting of the plastic material could be rolled across deserts to generate enough clean energy to supply the entire planet's power needs.
   Definition 1: **farms:** Land used to produce plants or animals for human use.

   Definition 2: ____

3. In Japan, the world's largest solar-power market, the government expects that 50 percent of residential power supply will come from solar power by 2030, up from a fraction of a percent today.
   Definition 1: **market:** A place where goods and services are bought and sold.

   Definition 2: ____

6 Freewriting Write without stopping for 20 minutes about your response to the article on pages 141–142 and your opinion of solar energy.

7 Gathering Information Collect information on current developments in energy technology or energy conservation. Organize your information on a poster that you can display in class. Collect photos, drawings, and diagrams as you do your research. Include information from each of these categories:

- Description of the developments and breakthroughs/how you got the information
- What it looks like/how it works
- Cost of production/cost of use
- How it compares to previous versions
- Public reaction
- Your opinion and predictions

8 Sharing Results Present the results of your research to the class. As you present, make sure the class understands how the device, technology, or development works. As you listen, make sure that you understand each presentation. Ask questions about anything you don't understand. This will help the presenter write the essay for this chapter.

Part 2 Focusing on Words and Phrases

Discussing Energy

1 Finding Meaning in Context Below are some words and expressions from "Spray-On Solar-Power Cells Are True Breakthrough" on pages 141–142. Find them in the passage. Notice their contexts—how they are used in a sentence—and try to guess their meanings. Then match the meanings below to the words and expressions. Write the letters on the lines.

Words and Expressions	Meanings
_____ **1.** composite (Line 26)	**a.** very small items
_____ **2.** convert (Line 10)	**b.** band; range; continuum
_____ **3.** cost-effectiveness (Line 52)	**c.** a combination of chemicals
_____ **4.** detect (Line 32)	**d.** beaming; giving off rays
_____ **5.** displace (Line 56)	**e.** prepared to accept

______ **6.** kilowatt-hour (Line 62)	**f.** change the nature of
______ **7.** particles (Line 31)	**g.** the relationship between price of something and its benefit(s)
______ **8.** radiant (Line 35)	**h.** take the place of
______ **9.** resigned to (the fact that) (Line 41)	**i.** a measurement of energy; 1,000 watts per hour
______ **10.** spectrum (Line 25)	**j.** find

DESCRIBING TECHNOLOGY

Find the following expressions used for describing technology in the article and study them. You can use them to describe how something looks, how it works, or its advantages, both current and in the future. *X* represents the technology item you are describing.

X {
- uses
- contains
- consist(s) of

Example:

The plastic material uses nanotechnology and contains the first solar cells able to harness the sun's invisible rays.

X {
- can/could be + past participle*
- can/could be harnessed
- can/could be used
- can/could be used to
- can/could be used as
- can/could be used by

*Passive voice: BE + past participle (*verb* + ed)

Example:

The plastic coating could be woven into a shirt and used to charge an item like a cell phone.

X {
- could
- could potentially
- has/have the potential to

Possibilities include

Ultimately,

Example:

Energy-saving plastic sheeting has the potential to turn the sun's power into a clean, green, convenient source of energy.

2 **Using Expressions** Now complete each sentence below with the correct form of one of the expressions. More than one expression may be correct in some sentences.

1. A solar water–heating system for a building ______________________________ two main parts: a solar collector and a storage tank.
2. Some solar water–heating systems ______________________________ fluids other than water.
3. Solar process–heating systems ______________________________ heat large commercial buildings.
4. The heat from a solar collector ______________________________ even ______________________________ provide energy for cooling a building.
5. Solar energy technologies ______________________________ benefit nations around the world.
6. ______________________________ solar energy technologies __________________ improve the quality of the air we breathe, offset greenhouse gas emissions, and stimulate the economy by creating jobs in the manufacturing and installation of solar energy systems.

—Adapted from U.S. Department of Energy, Solar Energy Basics and Solar Energy Technologies Program.

3 **Using New Words and Expressions** Use the new words and expressions to complete the following activities:

1. Write a summary of "Spray-On Solar-Power Cells Are True Breakthrough" using words and expressions from this section.
2. Write a paragraph about the breakthrough you researched in Part 1. Use words and expressions from this section.
3. Choose one of the following items and describe how it works and what it does. You may want to draw a diagram to accompany your explanation.
   - a light bulb
   - a water wheel
   - a gas stove

Part 3 Organizing and Developing Your Ideas

Describing Processes

Review Points

- One way to make a point in an essay is to show a causal relationship.
- There are several ways to organize a cause-effect essay.

New Points

- Writing that describes processes (often in scientific writing) requires careful organization.
- Chronological descriptions of processes use listing signals such as *first, second, next,* and *finally* to describe the steps the process involves.
- Structural descriptions of processes describe and/or analyze an object or event.
- The thesis statement in a process essay is often an announcement of what you are going to describe and how you will go about it.

PROCESS PARAGRAPHS

Read this example of a process paragraph that contains a chronological description.

There are several steps to follow in order to write a good essay in class. First, the writer must read the assignment very carefully and make sure he or she understands the topic. Second, the writer should jot down ideas that come to mind when thinking about the topic. Next, the writer should organize the notes and compose a thesis statement. The writer should plan how much time he or she should spend on each part of the essay and stick to the schedule carefully. Finally, after the essay is written, the writer must proofread carefully to catch mistakes.

Now read this example of a process paragraph that contains a structural description.

A solar cooker is made with plastic on a hoop laid over a parabolic concrete mound. It is lined with a mosaic of one-inch mirrors. The adjustable U-frame made of water pipe rotates around a pipe driven into the ground, and the reflecting shell is suspended from the horizontal pipe that supports the small circular grill for holding the cooking vessel. The frame is rotated, and the reflecting solar collector is tilted to bring the shadow of the kettle to the center of the collector by pulling a chain that can be caught over a protruding bolt in the frame.

—Adapted from Farrington Daniels, *Direct Use of the Sun's Energy.*

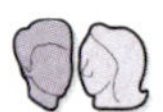

1 Describing a Process Describe for a partner a process that you are familiar with, but that he or she may not be familiar with. It can be scientific or nonscientific. You might consider some of the following: how to do something using personal electronics such as texting on your cell phone or sending a fax; how to cook your favorite dish; or how to buy a used car. Read each other's descriptions. Are they clear? Easy to follow?

2 Practicing What You've Learned Practice what you've learned about describing processes in the following activities:

1. In a paragraph, describe one of the following mechanisms, including its parts, the position of its parts, and how it is used.
   - a pulley
   - a mechanical pencil
   - a pair of scissors
   - an eyedropper
2. In a paragraph, describe the parts of a device or machine that you are familiar with and how the device or machine operates.

TOEFL® IBT

Focus on Testing

Listing Signals in Writing for Standardized Tests

The listing signals you just learned are useful in only a few kinds of writing tasks on the TOEFL® (iBT). Overusing these signals may cause some raters to think you have a very limited vocabulary for transitions. It is important to recognize which kinds of prompts allow listing and which do not.

Listing signals are most valuable when the prompt asks you simply to name some reasons, methods, or other ideas that can be counted. These ideas are usually equal in importance and usually have no relationships to each other except for being part of the same list. If more complex relationships exist between ideas, listing signals are not strong enough to show those.

Here are some typical TOEFL® (iBT) prompts that allow for listing:

1. Using information from both the reading and the lecture, name several ways in which hot spots in the earth are different from fracture zones.
2. Would you prefer to be supported at school by the government or by your family? Why?
3. In what ways does the lecture cast doubt on the reading's statements about the fragility of the Arctic tundra?

Sample prompt 1 could be answered by a list of differences: *One difference....Another difference...Thirdly,....*and so on.

Sample prompt 2, which asks *why?*, could be answered with a list of reasons: *One reason is...For another thing...A third reason is...*and so on.

Sample prompt 3 could be answered with a list of ways: *An obvious way is...Secondly...Yet another way is...*and so on.

Other prompts require transitions to show relationships such as cause-effect *(As a result...This led to...,* etc.), making possible *(Under these conditions..., With all the trees cut from the hillside...,* etc.), concession *(However..., Although...)*, or contrast *(On the other hand..., Unlike the reading,...,* etc).

Practice: Read each prompt below and put a checkmark (✔) in the blank of any prompt that could be answered by using a listing signal. Be prepared to explain to other students or to the class as a whole why you answered as you did.

1. _____ Explain how the author's point of view differs from the lecturer's.

2. _____ Describe an incident in which a friend helped you overcome a problem at school.

3. _____ Using information from both the reading and the lecture, explain how invasive species have entered the Great Lakes ecosystem.

Writing Product

3 Writing About a Development in Energy Conservation

Write an essay on the following topic using the ideas that you've discussed and written about so far in this chapter.

Describe an important energy conservation development.

Part 4 Evaluating Your Writing

Use the following rubric to score your writing. Read the rubric with your class, then give your writing a score. A classmate and a teacher will score your writing also and explain reasons for their scores. If you want to revise and improve this essay or writing from a previous chapter, you can do it now.

Rubric for Describing an Important Energy Conservation Development

Score	Description
3 **Excellent**	■ **Content:** Writing presents an important energy conservation development and explains clearly why it is important and how it conserves energy. ■ **Organization:** Ideas are organized to support and explain main idea through an introduction, a main idea, body paragraphs, and a conclusion; ideas follow a logical sequence and are easy to follow. ■ **Vocabulary and Sentence Structure:** Vocabulary is specific and descriptive; sentence types are varied. ■ **Grammar:** Subjects and verbs agree; common grammar problems (pronouns, articles, and plurals) are minimal so that meaning is clear. ■ **Spelling and Mechanics:** Most words are spelled correctly and punctuation is correct.
2 **Adequate**	■ **Content:** Writing presents an energy conservation development and explains how it conserves energy, although the reader may have questions. ■ **Organization:** Ideas are organized and there is a clear beginning, middle, and end; main idea is clear; some parts may be undeveloped. ■ **Vocabulary and Sentence Structure:** Vocabulary is descriptive; sentences are mostly the same type. ■ **Grammar:** Subjects and verbs mostly agree; common grammar problems (pronouns, articles, and plurals) are distracting. ■ **Spelling and Mechanics:** There are some distracting spelling and/or punctuation mistakes.

1 **Developing**	▪ **Content:** Writing does not present an energy conservation development clearly or sufficiently. ▪ **Organization:** Ideas do not follow essay format and are confusing or too brief. ▪ **Vocabulary and Sentence Structure:** Vocabulary is limited and/or there are too many mistakes to understand and/or to follow the ideas; sentences have mistakes. ▪ **Grammar:** Many common grammar problems (pronouns, articles, and plurals) are confusing to the reader. ▪ **Spelling and Mechanics:** There are many distracting spelling and/or punctuation mistakes.

Self-Assessment Log

In this chapter, you worked through the following activities. How much did they help you become a better writer? Check *A lot*, *A little*, or *Not at all*.

	A lot	A little	Not at all
I discussed solar-powered devices with my classmates.	❑	❑	❑
I read about an innovation in solar power.	❑	❑	❑
I learned how to expand beyond the literal meaning of words.	❑	❑	❑
I gathered and shared information about energy technology.	❑	❑	❑
I learned and used vocabulary for writing about energy and technology.	❑	❑	❑
I described a process in my essay.	❑	❑	❑
I evaluated my essay.	❑	❑	❑
(Add something) ____________________	❑	❑	❑

Chapter 9

Art and Entertainment

In This Chapter

Genre Focus: Interpretation

Writing Product

In this chapter, you'll write about a work of art.

Writing Process

- Discuss works of art.
- Read about art and nature.
- Apply what you've learned to new situations.
- Gather information about art and artists.
- Learn and use vocabulary for describing and analyzing art.
- Write introductions and conclusions.

"All art is an individual's expression of a culture. Cultures differ, so art looks different."

—Henry Glassie
Professor of Folklore and American Civilization (1941–)

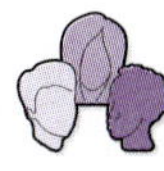

Connecting to the Topic

1. Who is your favorite artist?
2. What kind of art do you like?
3. What is your favorite work of art? Why is it your favorite?

Part 1 Preparing to Write

Getting Started

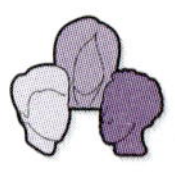

1 Discussing Works of Art Look at the following works of art, then answer the questions that follow.

▲ Cave painting (Spain) 13,000 BCE

▲ *Working in the Rice Fields,* Hyo Chong Yoo.

▲ *California Scenario,* Isamu Noguchi (United States) 1980–1982

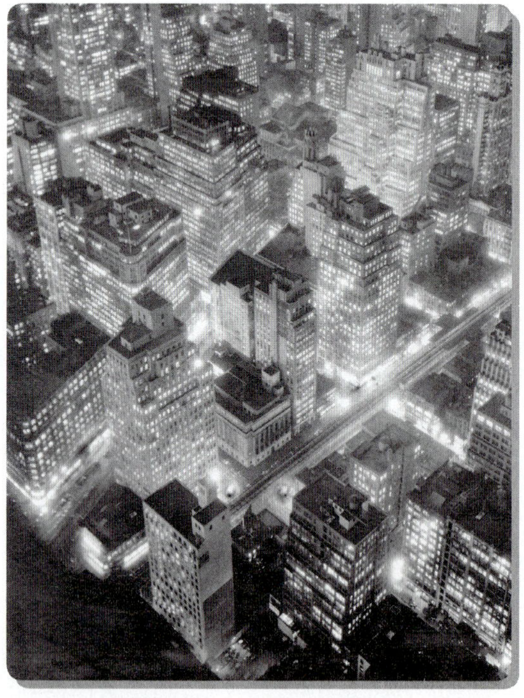

▲ *Nightview, New York*, Berenice Abbot (United States) 1932.

Chinese landscape painting

overlook: ____________________

pavilions: ____________________

rambling: ____________________

***Rock Garden at* Ryoan-ji Temple**

earthen: ____________________

gravel: ____________________

viewing platform: ____________________

Strategy

Thinking Critically: *Applying What You've Learned*

Applying what you've learned to another situation helps you understand it better. In the passage, you learned how works of art can sometimes show you what is important to the artist or to the culture in which the artist lives.

5 Applying What You've Learned Think about a work of art that you know or use one of the pictures on page 154, and explain what it might say about what is important to the artist or to the artist's culture.

6 Freewriting Write for 20 minutes without stopping about your favorite work of art. It can be a photograph, a painting, a sculpture, a garden, or a building. Explain what it says about the person who created it or about the culture that it was created in.

7 Gathering Information Find out more information about one of the aspects of art discussed in this chapter. Choose one of the following:

- A particular artist (for example, Thomas Cole)
- A particular work of art (for example, *The Oxbow*)
- A particular type of art (for example, landscape art)
- A particular culture's artistic traditions (for example, Chinese)

Get as much information as you can by doing Internet or library research. Write a one- to three-page summary of the information. Make copies of the work or works of art you are discussing to support your information.

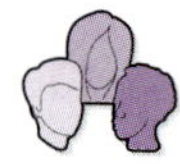

8 **Sharing Results** Share your findings from the preceding activity with your classmates. Present your research in small groups or to the entire class. Make sure you bring copies of the artwork to show your classmates.

Your presentation should take five to ten minutes. Organize it as you do an essay, with an introduction, a body, and a conclusion. As you listen to the other presentations, take notes, because you may be able to use the information in your writing assignment for this chapter.

Part 2 Focusing on Words and Phrases

Describing and Analyzing Art

1 **Finding Meaning in Context** Below are some words and expressions from "Themes and Purposes of Art: Art and Nature" on pages 156–157. Find them in the passage. Notice their contexts—how they are used in a sentence—and try to guess their meanings. Then match the meanings below to the words and expressions. Write the letters on the lines.

Words and Expressions	Meanings
_____ **1.** canvas (Line 25)	**a.** shows the difference between
_____ **2.** construct of the mind (Line 27)	**b.** look at
_____ **3.** embody (Line 41)	**c.** not wild
_____ **4.** emerging into (Lines 16–17)	**d.** inheritance
_____ **5.** depicted (Line 12)	**e.** painting
_____ **6.** draws a distinction between (Line 43)	**f.** something imagined
_____ **7.** heritage (Line 11)	**g.** represent
_____ **8.** in the mind's eye (Line 32)	**h.** coming into
_____ **9.** survey (Line 46)	**i.** in the imagination
_____ **10.** tamed (Line 43)	**j.** showed

EXPRESSIONS TO DESCRIBE ART

The expressions on page 161 can be used to describe what you see in a work of art. You can also use them to explain the message of the work of art; that is, the ideas behind the art.

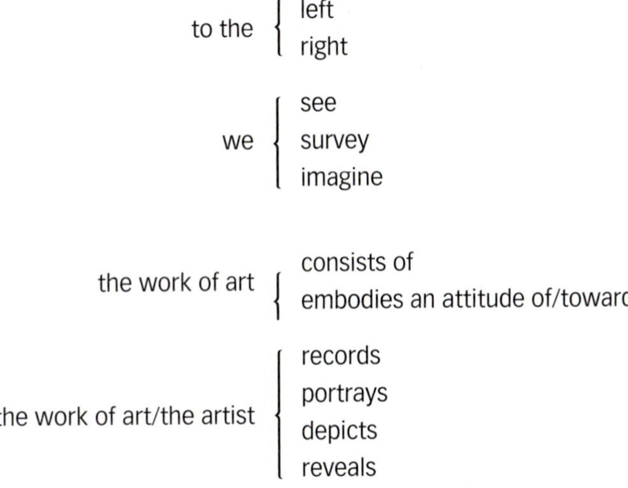

to the { left / right }

we { see / survey / imagine }

the work of art { consists of / embodies an attitude of/toward }

the work of art/the artist { records / portrays / depicts / reveals }

---

2 **Using Expressions** Find the expressions above in the reading passage. Then complete the sentences with the correct forms of the expressions above. More than one expression may be correct in some blanks.

1. Berenice Abbott's photograph, *Nightview, New York,* ______________________ the city at night.
2. *Nightview, New York* ______________________ an aerial view of brightly lit skyscrapers.
3. ______________________ we see a long boulevard that separates two city blocks.
4. In *Nightview, New York,* ______________________ the city from above, as though we are flying over it.
5. *Nightview, New York* ______________________ the city as a magical place, a sparkling fairyland.
6. *Nightview, New York* ______________________ a positive attitude toward a manufactured environment, a big city.

Paragraph Practice

3 **Using New Words and Expressions** Use the new words and expressions from this section to complete the following activities:

1. Describe one of the works of art in on page 154 using words and expressions from this section.
2. Describe the work of art from your research in Part 1 using words and expressions from this section.

Part 3 Organizing and Developing Your Ideas

Writing Introductions and Conclusions

Review Points

- An academic essay contains an introduction with a thesis statement, body paragraphs, and a conclusion.
- The purpose of the introduction is to make the reader interested in your topic.
- The conclusion summarizes your main points and tells the reader that you have completed the essay.

New Points

- An introduction in an academic essay prepares readers for what is to come and draws them into the essay by creating a high level of interest.
- Types of introductions that create a high level of interest include those that begin with background information, a quotation, a definition, or a summary.

INTRODUCTIONS

Read the following descriptions and examples of these four types of introductions:

1. *Background information.* Presents background on the topic that slowly leads up to the thesis. For example:

All of us have different styles of communicating with other people. Our style depends on a lot of things: where we're from, how and where we were raised, our educational background, and our age. It also can depend on our gender. Generally speaking, men and women talk differently, although there are varying degrees of masculine and feminine speech characteristics in each of us. But men and women do speak in very particular ways that are associated with gender.

2. *Quotation.* Must be directly related to the main idea of the essay; it can be from reading that you have done to prepare for your essay or it can be from a well-known saying, an appropriate remark from a famous person, or a line from a song or a poem. For example:

In an effort to create the right environment for students, educators constantly propose new ways to educate students. Some people, such as William O'Connor, insist: "We have no inferior education in our schools; what we have been getting is an inferior type of student." However, it is wrong to say that it is only the student who is inferior, not the school. One system is not appropriate for all students. Problems arise when students' individual needs are not met. Therefore, the needs of the students must be considered when deciding which system is best. Basically, there are three types of systems that are right for different students: an authoritarian system, a free system, and a combination of the two.

3. *Definition.* Prepares the reader for applications and examples of the concept or term being defined. For example:

Success is a term that has many meanings. For students, success can mean getting good grades or getting a good job after graduation. To a businessperson, success is making a lot of money and gaining a position of power. To an artist, however, success is having the ability to express inner feelings and having people recognize the artist's intentions.

4. *Summary.* Summarizes a reading selection (or a lecture or speech) and prepares the reader for an analysis or discussion of what has been summarized. For example:

In her article "African Art as Nonverbal Communication," Thelma Newman discusses African art and the inadequacy of European attempts to categorize it. Newman describes several characteristics common to most examples of African art and shows how these characteristics reveal a great deal about African culture. It is clear, therefore, that one can learn about the customs and values of a country by studying its art.

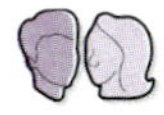

1 Practicing What You've Learned Rewrite four introductions from previous essays that you have written in this course. Use each of the four types of introductions described in this section. Exchange your new introduction with a partner and evaluate each other's work.

Writing Conclusions

New Points

- A good conclusion makes the reader feel that you have kept the promise of your thesis statement and that you are effectively bringing your essay to a close.
- One way to effectively bring an essay to a close is to leave the reader with a challenging or provocative thought on the topic by restating the main points of the essay and including some new information on the topic.
- The new information in this kind of conclusion can be a statement, a question, or your opinion about the essay topic (unless you've already expressed it elsewhere in the essay).

CONCLUSIONS

The following is an example of an effective conclusion. It is from the student essay in Chapter 1 "The Benefits of Online Language Learning," pages 16–17. Notice that in this conclusion the writer restates the main points of the essay and includes new information on the topic to challenge the reader.

The benefits of online self-study courses are that they are low-cost, people can do them at any time, and they can do them alone in the privacy of their own home or office. This last benefit is especially important in that many people feel less inhibited about acquiring and practicing language skills when they are alone. In addition, class size at many institutions limits the opportunities for foreign language students to get adequate individual attention. These are just a few of the reasons that an online course is a good way for many people to learn a foreign language.

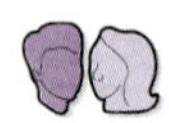

2 Practicing What You've Learned Find a conclusion from one of your previous essays that did not contain new information or ideas. Rewrite it so that it does contain new information or ideas. Exchange your new conclusion with a partner and evaluate each other's work.

TOEFL® iBT

Focus on Testing

Having a Repertoire of Introductions and Conclusions

Part 3 presents new ways to write introductions and conclusions. Having a repertoire (a collection) of two or three introduction and conclusion types will help you plan and write more quickly in test-taking situations.

Writing Product

3 Writing About a Work of Art Write an essay on the following topic. Use the ideas that you've discussed and written about so far in this chapter.

Describe a work of art and explain what it says about the artist or about what is important in the artist's culture.

Part 4 Evaluating Your Writing

Use the following rubric to score your writing. Read the rubric with your class, then give your writing a score. A classmate and a teacher will score your writing also and explain reasons for their scores. If you want to revise and improve this essay or writing from a previous chapter, you can do it now.

Rubric for Describing a Work of Art and What It Says About the Artist or the Artist's Culture

Score	Description
3 Excellent	■ **Content:** Writing describes a work of art and clearly explains how the art reveals information about the artist or the artist's culture. ■ **Organization:** Ideas are organized to support and explain main idea through an introduction, a main idea, body paragraphs, and a conclusion; ideas follow a logical sequence and are easy to follow. ■ **Vocabulary and Sentence Structure:** Vocabulary is specific and descriptive; sentence types are varied. ■ **Grammar:** Subjects and verbs agree; common grammar problems (pronouns, articles, and plurals) are minimal so that meaning is clear. ■ **Spelling and Mechanics:** Most words are spelled correctly, and punctuation is correct.

2 **Adequate**	▪ **Content:** Writing describes a work of art and explains how the art reveals information about the artist or the artist's culture though the reader may have questions. ▪ **Organization:** Ideas are organized and there is a clear beginning, middle, and end; main idea is clear; some parts may be undeveloped. ▪ **Vocabulary and Sentence Structure:** Vocabulary is descriptive; sentences are mostly the same type. ▪ **Grammar:** Subjects and verbs mostly agree; common grammar problems (pronouns, articles, and plurals) are distracting. ▪ **Spelling and Mechanics:** Some distracting spelling and/or punctuation mistakes.
1 **Developing**	▪ **Content:** Writing does not present a work of art or sufficiently explain how the art reveals information about the artist or the artist's culture. ▪ **Organization:** Ideas do not follow essay format and are confusing or too brief. ▪ **Vocabulary and Sentence Structure:** Vocabulary is limited and/or there are too many mistakes to understand and/or follow the ideas; sentences have mistakes. ▪ **Grammar:** Many common grammar problems (pronouns, articles, and plurals) that are confusing to the reader. ▪ **Spelling and Mechanics:** Many distracting spelling and/or punctuation mistakes.

Self-Assessment Log

In this chapter, you worked through the following activities. How much did they help you become a better writer? Check *A lot, A little,* or *Not at all*.

	A lot	**A little**	**Not at all**
I discussed works of art with my classmates.	❑	❑	❑
I read about art and nature.	❑	❑	❑
I applied what I learned to new situations.	❑	❑	❑
I gathered and shared information about art and artists.	❑	❑	❑
I learned and used vocabulary for describing and analyzing works of art.	❑	❑	❑
I wrote introductions and conclusions.	❑	❑	❑
I evaluated my essay.	❑	❑	❑
(Add something) ______________________________ ______________________________	❑	❑	❑

Chapter 10

Conflict and Reconciliation

In This Chapter

Genre Focus: Argument

Writing Product

In this chapter, you'll write about solutions to a conflict.

Writing Process

- Discuss photos of conflicts.
- Read about a solution to one kind of problem.
- Interpret metaphors.
- Learn and use vocabulary for discussing problems and solutions.
- Organize and develop a problem-solution essay.

"Mankind must find a method to resolve human conflict that rejects revenge, aggression, and retaliation. The foundation of such a method is love."

—Martin Luther King, Jr.
American Baptist minister and civil rights leader (1929–1968)

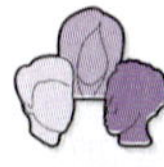

Connecting to the Topic

1. What are some problems in the world today?
2. What are some solutions to these problems?
3. What can the average person do to help to solve some of these problems?

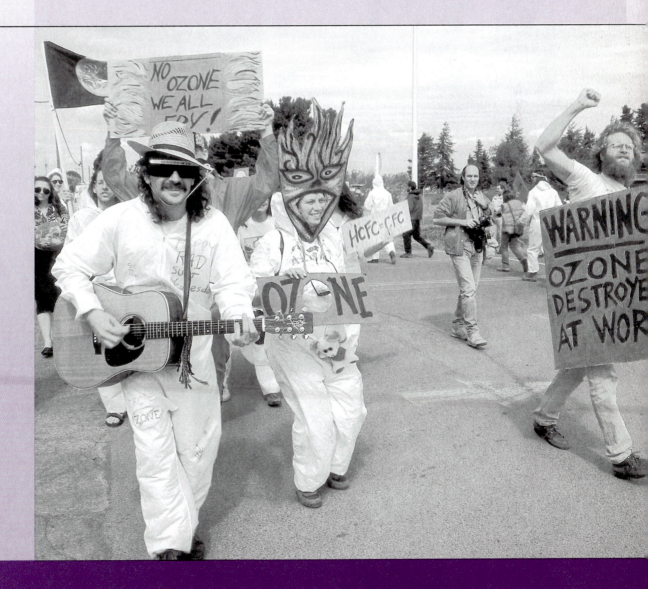

Part 1 Preparing to Write

Getting Started

1 Discussing Conflicts and Solutions Look at the following pictures and consider the conflicts (issues about which people disagree) each one shows. What are the two sides of each issue? (There may be more than two sides.) Is there a solution? What might make both sides happy? Complete the chart that follows.

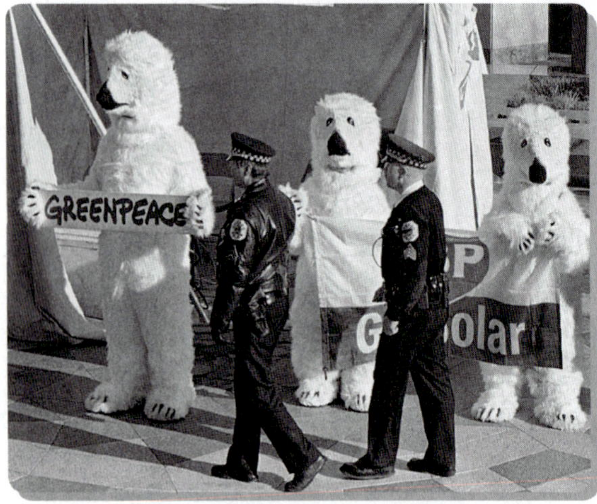

▲ 1. Greenpeace is an international organization that promotes wildlife and environmental protection

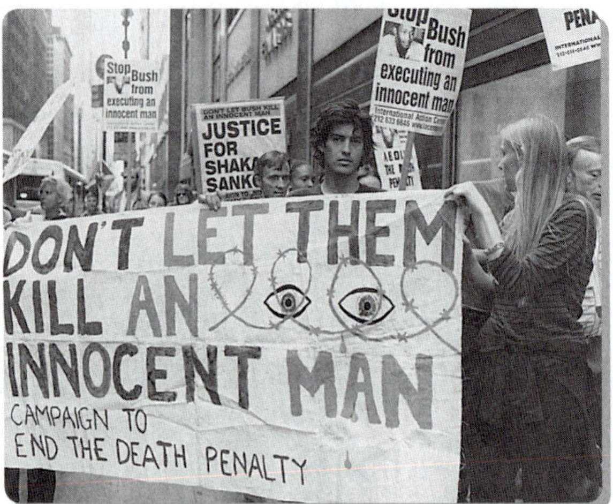

▲ 2. People protesting the death penalty

▲ 3. People protesting animal research

Photo	What is the conflict?	What are the different sides of the issue?	What is one solution?

▲ Gary Snyder

2 Preparing to Read Gary Snyder is an American poet who was born in San Francisco in 1930. His work reflects his studies of Eastern philosophy and his commitment to environmental issues. The following selections (a speech and a poem) are from his book *Turtle Island.* Answer the questions at the top of page 172 before you read.

1. Is the environment in danger? If yes, what are some of the problems? What are some of the causes of these problems? What are some of the solutions?

____

____

____

2. What can we learn from nature?

____

____

Turtle Island (Selections)

I. Speech

A I am a poet. My teachers are other poets, American Indians, and a few Buddhist priests in Japan. The reason I am here is because I wish to bring a voice from the wilderness, my constituency. I wish to be a spokesman for a realm that is not usually represented either in intellectual chambers or in the chambers of government.

B I would like to think of a new definition of humanism and a new definition of democracy that would include the nonhuman, that would have representation from those spheres. This is what I think we mean by an ecological conscience.

C I don't like Western culture because I think it has much in it that is inherently wrong and that is at the root of the environmental crisis that is not recent; it is very ancient; it has been building up for a millennium. There are many things in Western culture that are admirable. But a culture that alienates itself from the very ground of its own being—from the wilderness outside (that is to say, wild nature, the wild, self-contained, self-informing, ecosystems) and from that other wilderness, the wilderness within—is doomed to a very destructive behavior, ultimately perhaps self-destructive behavior.

D The West is not the only culture that carries these destructive seeds. China had effectively deforested itself by AD 800. The soils of the Middle East were ruined even earlier. The forests that once covered the mountains of Yugoslavia were stripped to build the Roman fleet, and those mountains have looked like Utah ever since. The soils of southern Italy and Sicily were ruined by slave-labor farming in the Roman Empire. The soils of the Atlantic seaboard in the United States were effectively ruined before the American Revolution because of the one-crop (tobacco) farming. So the same forces have been at work in East and West.

E A line is drawn between primitive peoples and civilized peoples. I think there is a wisdom in the world view of primitive peoples that we have to refer ourselves to and learn from. If we are on the verge of post-civilization, then our next step must take account of the primitive world view which has traditionally and intelligently tried to keep open lines of communication with the forces of nature. You cannot communicate with the forces of nature in a laboratory. One of the problems is that we simply do not know much about primitive people and primitive cultures. If we can tentatively accommodate the possibility that nature has a degree of authenticity and intelligence that requires that we look at it more sensitively, then we can move on to the next step.

II. For the Children (poem)

F The rising hills, the slopes,
of statistics
lie before us.
The steep climb
of everything, going up,
up, as we all
go down.
In the next century
or the one beyond that,
they say,
are valleys, pastures,
we can meet there in peace
if we make it.
To climb these coming
crests one word to you,
to you and your children:
stay together
learn the flowers
go light

—Gary Snyder, *Turtle Island*

3 Understanding the Reading In small groups, answer these questions.

1. Who or what does Snyder want to be a "spokesman" for?

____

2. According to Snyder, what is one thing that is wrong with Western culture?

____

3. What is Snyder's view of "primitive" people?

____

____

4. In his speech, what conflict does Snyder discuss? Who is it between?

____

____

5. In "For the Children," Snyder offers hope for a reconciliation of (a solution to) the conflict. What advice does he give for helping this reconciliation to happen?

____

6. Do you agree with Snyder's ideas? Why or why not?

____

____

Strategy

Thinking Critically: *Interpreting Metaphors*

A metaphor is a word or phrase that describes something by comparing it to something else without using the words *like* or *as.* Many writers use metaphors. In "For the Children," Snyder compares elements of nature to information. He writes:

> The rising hills, the slopes,
> of statistics
> lie before us.

4 Practicing Interpreting Metaphors In small groups, read Gary Snyder's poem on page 173 again. What do the words *hills* and *valleys* represent? Share your ideas and discuss the reasons for your interpretations. There are no right or wrong answers—many interpretations are possible.

5 Freewriting Write for 20 minutes without stopping about a conflict that interests you. Describe the different sides of the issue and propose one or more solutions.

6 Sharing Information In a small group, discuss the conflicts you wrote about in Activity 5. Take notes on the conflicts using the chart on the next page:

What is the conflict?	What are the different sides of the issue?	What is one solution?

7 Solving a Problem by Consensus Fire Mountain is a small community in the southwestern United States. Read the following passage, which describes a conflict the residents are trying to resolve.

> Fire Mountain is a scenic area that attracts many hikers and tourists every year. It is famous for its ancient Native American dwellings and varied wildlife. Fire Mountain also contains a rich supply of coal. Winters are cold, so the people near Fire Mountain need an inexpensive and steady supply of fuel, which Fire Mountain could provide. In addition, there is a high unemployment rate in the area. If Fire Mountain were mined for coal, people could get work. The problem is that stripmining makes the land ugly and kills animals. How should the people at Fire Mountain solve this problem?

Work in small groups to propose a solution to the problem. Try to reach a consensus (come to an agreement) in your group, then present it to the class.

Part 2 Focusing on Words and Phrases

Discussing Problems and Solutions

1 Finding Meaning in Context Below are some words and expressions from "Turtle Island" on pages 172–173. Find them in the passage. Notice their contexts—how they are used in a sentence—and try to guess their meanings. Then match the meanings below to the words and expressions. Write the letters on the lines.

Words and Expressions	Meanings
_____ **1.** alienates itself from (Line 14)	**a.** basically
_____ **2.** authenticity (Line 36)	**b.** communities of living things and their environments
_____ **3.** voice from the wilderness (Line 3)	**c.** a philosophy of what it is to be human
_____ **4.** constituency (Line 3)	**d.** realness; being real
_____ **5.** ecological conscience (Lines 8–9)	**e.** when a civilized culture is no longer civilized.
_____ **6.** ecosystems (Line 16)	**f.** a group of people who are represented by someone
_____ **7.** humanism (Line 6)	**g.** cautiously
_____ **8.** inherently (Lines 9–10)	**h.** a sense of caring about the environment
_____ **9.** post-civilization (Line 30)	**i.** becomes a stranger to
_____ **10.** tentatively (Line 35)	**j.** a single voice; an opinion that not many share

Here are some expressions that Snyder uses to describe problems and solutions:

Problems

one of the problems is that . . .
the/a(n) [environmental] crisis
[something] BE at the root of destructive behavior
on the verge of . . .
[something] is doomed to

Solutions

If . . ., (then) . . .
Our/the next step is . . .
keep (open) lines of communication (open)
Note: *Open* is in one position, not both.

▲ A computer recycling center

2 **Finding Expressions** Find the expressions on the previous page in "Turtle Island" on pages 172–173. Notice the way each fits grammatically in a sentence.

3 **Using Expressions** Complete the paragraph below using the following list of expressions. More than one expression may be correct in some blanks.

destructive behavior	are doomed to
at the root of	one of the problems is that
an environmental crisis	if
the next step is	keep the lines of communication open

There are several problems with recycling obsolete computers in developing nations. ________ (1) old computers aren't actually recycled; rather, they are burned. Because computers contain many toxic substances, this burning is causing both a health and ________ (2) in some parts of the developing world. For example, burning discarded computers is ________ (3) the current air pollution problem in some parts of China. Poor air quality is causing health problems among the workers at these recycling plants, many of whom are women and children. These workers ________ (4) a life of poor health. What can we do about this ________ (5)? I propose a solution. ________ (6) computer manufacturers will take responsibility for the safe disposal of their products, this health and environmental crisis may be averted. ________ (7) to abolish the burning of computers in third world countries. If we can ________ (8) between computer users, computer manufacturers, and third world governments, we can solve this problem.

Paragraph Practice

4 Using New Words and Expressions Use the new words and expressions from this section to complete the following activities:

1. Write about one of the conflicts in the photos on page 170. Include as many words and expressions from this section as you can.
2. Develop your freewriting from Activity 5 on page 174 into a paragraph. Include as many words and expressions from this section as you can.

Part 3 Organizing and Developing Your Ideas

Discussing Problems and Solutions

Review Points

- A thesis statement previews an essay by presenting the writer's approach to the topic.
- The organizational pattern you choose for an essay depends on the topic of the essay.

New Points

- One way to make a point in an essay is to describe a problem and propose a solution.
- The thesis statement for a problem-solution essay mentions both the problem and the solution.
- You can describe a problem and propose a solution in a paragraph or in an entire essay.

1 Analyzing a Problem-Solution Thesis Statement Read the following example of a problem-solution thesis statement and answer the questions on the next page.

> Because exposure to discarded computers in the recycling process is extremely hazardous to human health, computer manufacturers must take responsibility for properly disposing of their own obsolete products, and developing nations must ban burning at recycling centers.

1. What is the problem? ______________________________

____

____

____

____

2. What if any solution(s) is (are) proposed? ______________________________

____

____

____

____

PROBLEM-SOLUTION ESSAY BASED ON A THESIS STATEMENT

Look again at the thesis statement above. When you read it, how do you expect the essay to be organized?

____

____

____

____

Here's one way to organize a problem-solution essay based on the thesis statement above:

I. Introduction + thesis statement
II. Describe the problem and propose the solutions
III. Solution #1
IV. Solution #2
V. Conclusion

2 Studying Problem-Solution Organizational Patterns Here's another problem-solution thesis statement. Draw one line under the problem and draw two lines under the proposed solution.

> We are facing serious environmental problems, such as pollution and endangered species, but there are simple things that the average person can do to help save the environment.

Notice that this thesis statement presents the problem and suggests a solution. However, the solution is general and may have more than one part.

PROBLEM-SOLUTION ESSAY WITH A GENERAL SOLUTION

Here's a way to organize a problem-solution essay with a general solution:

I. Introduction + thesis statement
II. Describe the problem and propose the solution
III. One aspect of the solution, for example, eating less overfished species
IV. Another aspect of the solution, for example, riding a bike one day a week
V. Another aspect of the solution, for example, stopping using pesticides
VI. Conclusion

---

3 Practicing What You've Learned Complete the following tasks to practice what you've learned about organizing problems and solutions.

1. Choose one of the conflicts in the photos on page 170. Write a thesis statement that expresses the problem and proposes two or more solutions.
Thesis Statement:

____

____

____

2. Choose one of the conflicts in the photos on page 170. Write a thesis statement that expresses the problem and proposes a general solution.
Thesis Statement:

____

____

____

3. Choose a problem or conflict that interests you. Write a thesis statement that expresses the problem and proposes one or more solutions.
Thesis Statement:

____

____

____

4. On a piece of paper, make an organizational pattern for the thesis statement you wrote in item 3. Then decide what information you would need to develop each paragraph and make notes on your organizational pattern.

Focus on Testing

Brainstorming to Get Started

Sometimes it is difficult to get started writing when you are under pressure. By quickly jotting down any ideas you have about the topic, you can overcome temporary writer's block. Brainstorming helps you collect vocabulary and gather knowledge.

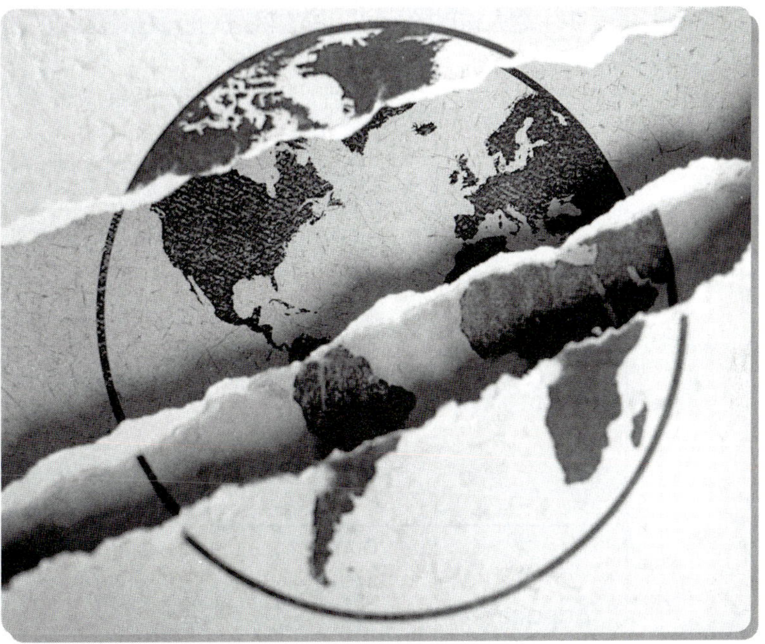

▲ A world in strife

Writing Product

4 Writing About Conflict Write an essay on the following topic. Use the ideas you've discussed and the material you've written so far in this chapter and previous chapters as the basis for your essay.

> Choose a current conflict that you consider important. Write an essay in which you explain the conflict or problem and propose one or more solutions.

Part 4 Evaluating Your Writing

Use the following rubric to score your writing. Read the rubric with your class, then give your writing a score. A classmate and a teacher will score your writing also and explain reasons for their scores. If you want to revise and improve this essay or writing from a previous chapter, you can do it now.

Rubric for Writing About a Problem and One or More Solutions

Score	Description
3 **Excellent**	▪ **Content:** Writing describes a problem clearly and explains convincingly how the problem can be solved. ▪ **Organization:** Writing includes an introduction, body paragraphs that present the problem and explain solutions, and a conclusion; ideas follow a logical sequence and are easy to follow. ▪ **Vocabulary and Sentence Structure:** Vocabulary is specific, descriptive, and persuasive; sentence types are varied. ▪ **Grammar:** Subjects and verbs agree; common grammar problems (pronouns, articles, and plurals) are minimal so that meaning is clear. ▪ **Spelling and Mechanics:** Most words are spelled correctly and punctuation is correct.
2 **Adequate**	▪ **Content:** Writing describes a problem and explains one or more solutions, although the reader may have questions. ▪ **Organization:** Ideas are organized and there is a clear beginning, middle, and end; some parts may be undeveloped. ▪ **Vocabulary and Sentence Structure:** Vocabulary is descriptive; sentences are mostly of the same type. ▪ **Grammar:** Subjects and verbs mostly agree; common grammar problems (pronouns, articles, and plurals) are distracting. ▪ **Spelling and Mechanics:** There are some distracting spelling and/or punctuation mistakes.

1 **Developing**	■ **Content:** Writing does not present a problem or sufficiently explain a solution. ■ **Organization:** Ideas do not follow essay format and are confusing or too brief. ■ **Vocabulary and Sentence Structure:** Vocabulary is limited and/or there are too many mistakes to understand and/or follow the ideas; sentences have mistakes. ■ **Grammar:** Many common grammar problems (pronouns, articles, and plurals) are confusing to the reader. ■ **Spelling and Mechanics:** There are many distracting spelling and/or punctuation mistakes.

Self-Assessment Log

In this chapter, you worked through the following activities. How much did they help you become a better writer? Check *A lot, A little,* or *Not at all.*

	A lot	A little	Not at all
I discussed photos of conflicts with my classmates.	❑	❑	❑
I read about a solution to one kind of problem.	❑	❑	❑
I learned how to interpret metaphors.	❑	❑	❑
I learned and used vocabulary for discussing problems and solutions.	❑	❑	❑
I organized and developed a problem-solution essay.	❑	❑	❑
I evaluated my essay.	❑	❑	❑
(Add something) ________________________________ ________________________________	❑	❑	❑

Appendix 1

Spelling Rules for Adding Endings

Endings That Begin with Vowels (*-ed, -ing, -er, -est*)

1. For words ending in silent *e*, drop the *e* and add the ending.

   lik**e** → lik**ed**   mak**e** → mak**ing**   saf**e** → saf**er**   fin**e** → fin**est**

2. For one-syllable words ending in a single vowel and a single consonant, double the final consonant, and add the ending.

   b**at** → bat**ted**   **run** → run**ning**   f**at** → fat**ter**   h**ot** → hot**test**

3. Don't double the final consonant when the word has two final consonants or two vowels before a final consonant.

   pi**ck** → pic**ked**   sin**g** → sin**ging**   cl**ea**n → clea**ner**   c**oo**l → cool**est**

4. For words of two or more syllables that end in a single vowel and a single consonant, double the final consonant if the stress is on the final syllable.

   ref**er** → refer**red**   beg**in** → begin**ning**   beg**in** → begin**ner**

5. For words of two or more syllables that end in a single vowel and a single consonant, make no change if the stress is not on the final syllable.

   trav**el** → trave**led**   trav**el** → trave**ling**
   trav**el** → trave**ler**   yell**ow** → yell**owest**

6. For words ending in a consonant and *y*, change the *y* to *i* and add the ending unless the ending begins with *i*.

   stu**dy** → stud**ied**   dirt**y** → dirt**ier**   sunn**y** → sunn**iest**
   stu**dy** → stud**ying**   hurr**y** → hurr**ying**

7. For words ending in a vowel and *y*, make no change before adding the ending.

   pl**ay** → play**ed**   st**ay** → stay**ing**   pl**ay** → play**er**   gr**ay** → gray**est**

Endings That Begin with Consonants (*-ly, -ment*)

1. For words ending in a silent *e*, make no change when adding endings that begin with consonants.

   fin**e** → fin**ely**   stat**e** → stat**ement**

2. For words ending in a consonant and *y*, change the *y* to *i* before adding the ending.

   hap**py** → happ**ily**   mer**ry** → merr**iment**

Adding a Final *s* to Nouns and Verbs

1. Generally, add the *s* without making changes.

   sit → sit**s** dance → dance**s** play → play**s** book → book**s**

2. If a word ends in a consonant and *y*, change the *y* to *i* and add *es*.

   mar**ry** → marr**ies** stu**dy** → stud**ies** cher**ry** → cherr**ies**

3. If word ends in *ch*, *s*, *sh*, *x*, or *z*, add *es*.

   chur**ch** → church**es** ca**sh** → cash**es** fiz**z** → fizz**es**
   bos**s** → boss**es** mi**x** → mix**es**

4. For words ending in *o*, sometimes add *es* and sometimes add *s*.

   tomat**o** → tomato**es** potat**o** → potato**es**
   pian**o** → piano**s** radi**o** → radio**s**

5. For words ending in *f* or *fe*, generally drop the *f* or *fe* and add *ves*.

   hal**f** → hal**ves** kni**fe** → kni**ves**

   Exceptions: sa**fe** → safe**s** roo**f** → roof**s**

Appendix 2

Capitalization Rules

First Words

1. Capitalize the first word of every sentence.

   They live near my house. **W**hat is it?

2. Capitalize the first word of a quotation that is a full sentence.

   He said, "**M**y name is Paul." Jenny asked, "**W**hen is the party?"

Personal Names

1. Capitalize the names of people including initials and titles.

   Mrs. **J**ones **M**ohandas **G**andhi **J**ohn **F**. **K**ennedy

2. Capitalize family words if they appear alone or followed by a name.

   Let's go, **D**ad. Where's **G**randma? She's at **A**unt **L**ucy's.

3. Don't capitalize family words with a possessive pronoun or article.

   my **u**ncle her **m**other our **g**randparents an **a**unt

4. Capitalize the pronoun *I*.

   I have a book. She's bigger than **I** am.

5. Capitalize the names of nationalities, races, peoples, and religions.

   Japanese **A**rab **A**sian **C**hicano **M**uslim

6. Generally, don't capitalize occupations.

   I am a **s**ecretary. She wants to be a **l**awyer.

Place Names

1. Capitalize the names of countries, states, provinces, and cities.

   Lebanon **N**ew **Y**ork **Q**uebec **I**stanbul

2. Capitalize the names of oceans, lakes, rivers, islands, and mountains.

   the **A**tlantic **O**cean **L**ake **C**omo the **N**ile **R**iver
   Maui **M**t. **A**rarat

3. Capitalize the names of geographical areas.

   the **S**outh the **M**iddle **E**ast **A**frica **A**ntarctica

4. Don't capitalize directions if they aren't names of geographical areas.

   He lives **e**ast of Toronto. We walked **s**outhwest.

5. Capitalize names of schools, parks, buildings, and streets.

   the **U**niversity of **G**eorgia **C**entral **P**ark
   the **S**ears **B**uilding **O**xford **R**oad

Time Words

1. Capitalize names of days and months.

   Monday **F**riday **J**anuary **M**arch

2. Capitalize names of holidays and historical events.

   Independence **D**ay **W**orld **W**ar II

3. Don't capitalize names of seasons.

   spring **s**ummer **f**all **w**inter

Titles

1. Capitalize the first word and all important words of titles of books, magazines, newspapers, songs, and articles.

   Interactions *The New York Times* "**T**raveling in **E**gypt"

2. Capitalize the first word and all important words in titles of movies, plays, radio programs, and television programs.

   *The **M**atrix* *The **T**empest* *News **R**oundup* *The **S**impsons*

3. Don't capitalize articles (*a*, *an*, *the*) conjunctions (*but*, *and*, *or*) or short prepositions (*of*, *with*, *in*, *on*, *for*) unless they are the first word of a title.
   *The Life **of** Pi* *War **and** Peace* *Death **of a** Salesman*

Names of Organizations

1. Capitalize the names of organizations, government groups, and businesses.

   International **S**tudent **A**ssociation   the **S**enate   **G**oogle™

2. Capitalize brand names, but do not capitalize the names of the product.

   IBM™ computer   **T**oyota™ truck   **K**ellogg's™ cereal

Other

1. Capitalize the names of languages.

   Arabic   **S**panish   **T**hai   **J**apanese

2. Don't capitalize school subjects unless they are the names of languages or are followed by a number.

   geometry   **m**usic   **E**nglish   **W**riting 101   **H**istory 211

Appendix 3

Punctuation Rules

Period

1. Use a period after a statement or command.

   We are studying English.   Open your books to Chapter 3.

2. Use a period after most abbreviations.

   Mr.   Ms.   Dr.   Ave.   etc.

3. Use a period after initials.

   H. G. Wells   Dr. H. R. Hammond

Question Mark

1. Use a question mark after (not before) questions.

   Where are you going?   Is he here yet?

2. In a direct quotation, the question mark goes before the quotation marks.

   He asked, "What's your name?"

Exclamation Point

Use an exclamation point after exclamatory sentences or phrases.

Let the students vote!   Be quiet!   Wow!

*In academic writing, exclamation points are very rare.

Comma

1. Use a comma before a conjunction (*and*, *or*, *so*, *but*) that separates two independent clauses.

   She wanted to work, so she decided to study English.
   He wasn't happy in his apartment, but he didn't have the money to move.

2. Don't use a comma before a conjunction that separates two phrases that aren't complete sentences.

   She worked in the library and studied at night.
   Do you want to go to a movie or stay home?

3. Use a comma after an introductory phrase (generally, if it is five or more words long).

   During the long summer vacation, I decided to learn Chinese.
   After a beautiful wedding ceremony, they had a reception in her mother's home.

   If you want to write well, you should practice often.

4. Use a comma to separate interrupting expressions from the rest of a sentence.

   Do you know, by the way, what time dinner is?
   Many of the students, I found out, stayed on campus during the holidays.

5. Use a comma after transition words and phrases.

   In addition, he stole all her jewelry.
   Common transitional words and phrases are:

also	for this reason	in addition	on the other hand
besides	for instance	in fact	similarly
consequently	furthermore	moreover	therefore
for example	however	nevertheless	

6. Use a comma to separate names of people in direct address from the rest of a sentence.

   Jane, have you seen Paul?
   We aren't sure where he is, Ms. Green.

7. Use a comma after *yes* and *no* in answers.

   Yes, he was here a minute ago.
   No, I haven't.

8. Use a comma to separate items in a series.

   We have coffee, tea, and milk.
   He looked in the refrigerator, on the shelves, and in the cupboard.

9. Use a comma to separate an appositive from the rest of a sentence.

   Mrs. Sampson, his English teacher, gave him a bad grade.
   Would you like to try a taco, a delicious Mexican food?

10. If a date or address has two or more parts, use a comma after each part.

    I was born on June 5, 1968.
    The house at 230 Seventh Street, Miami, Florida is for sale.

11. Use a comma to separate contrasting information from the rest of the sentence.

    It wasn't Jamila, but Fatima, who was absent.
    Bring your writing book, not your reading book.

12. Use a comma to separate quotations from the rest of a sentence.

    He asked, "What are we going to do?"
    "I didn't have enough money," she explained.

13. Use a comma to separate two or more adjectives that each modify the noun alone.

    She was an intelligent, beautiful actress. (*intelligent* and *beautiful* actress)
    Eat those delicious green beans. (*delicious* modifies *green beans*)

14. Use a comma to separate nonrestrictive clauses from the rest of a sentence. A nonrestrictive clause gives more information about the noun it describes, but it isn't needed to identify the noun. Clauses after proper names are nonrestrictive and require commas.

    It's a Wonderful Life, which is often on television at Christmas time, is my favorite movie.
    James Stewart, who plays a depressed man thinking of ending his life, received an Academy Award for his performance.

Semicolons

1. A semicolon is often an alternative to a period. Use a semicolon between two sentences that are very closely related.

   I'm sure Dan is at home; he never goes out on school nights.

2. Use a semicolon before transition words and phrases such as *however*, *therefore*, *nevertheless*, *furthermore*, *for example*, *as a result*, *that is*, and *in fact*.

   Malaria is a major health problem around the world; however, some progress is being made in developing low-cost treatments for it.

Quotation Marks

1. Use quotation marks at the beginning and end of exact quotations. Other punctuation marks go before the end quotation marks.

   He said, "I'm going to Montreal."
   "How are you traveling to France?" he asked.

2. Use quotation marks before and after titles of works that appear within larger works: short stories, articles, and songs. Periods and commas go before the final quotation marks.

   My favorite song is "Let it Be."

Apostrophes

1. Use apostrophes in contractions.

   don't it's* we've they're

*Notice the difference between: It's hot. (*It's* is a contraction of *it is*.)
The dog is hurt. Its leg is broken. (*Its* is possessive.)

2. Use an apostrophe to make possessive nouns.

   Singular: Jerry's my boss's
   Plural: the children's the Smiths'

Underlining and Italicizing

The tiles of books, magazines, newspapers, plays, television programs, and movies should be italicized. If italicizing is not possible because you are writing by hand, underline instead.

I am reading *One Hundred Years of Solitude.*
Did you like the movie *Crash*?

Appendix 4

A List of Noncount Nouns

Food

bread, butter, cheese, chicken*, chocolate, coffee,* cream, fish,* flour, fruit, ice cream,* juice, meat, milk, rice, salt, spaghetti, sugar, tea

Activities and Sports

baseball,* chess, dance,* skating, soccer, tennis

* These nouns have both count and noncount uses. They are noncount when they refer to the item in general. They are count when they refer to a particular item.

I love chicken. (the meat)
The farmer raised twenty chickens. (the animals)
Coffee is delicious. (the drink)
Can I have a coffee please? (a cup of coffee)

Natural Phenomena

Weather:	rain, snow, sunshine, thunder, wind
Gases:	air, hydrogen, nitrogen, oxygen
Minerals:	copper, gold, iron, silver, steel
Materials:	dirt, dust, grass, ice, land, oil, sand, water

Emotions and Qualities**

ambition, anger, courage, fear, freedom, happiness, hatred, honesty, justice, loneliness, love, joy, pride

Social Issues**

abortion, crime, democracy, divorce, freedom, hunger, nuclear power, peace, pollution, poverty

Mass Nouns (Composed of Dissimilar items)

change, clothing, fruit, equipment, furniture, information, jewelry, luggage, mail, machinery, makeup, medicine, money, noise, scenery, technology, transportation, vocabulary

Subjects

art, economics, history, humanities, physics

Miscellaneous

advice, business, fun, glass, homework, knowledge, information, insurance, life, nature, news, paint, publicity, reality, research, sleep, time, traffic, trouble, tuition, work

** Most emotions, qualities, and social issue nouns can also function as count nouns: a strong ambition, a deep hatred, a terrible crime, a young democracy

Appendix 5

Subordinating Conjunctions

Subordinating conjunctions can show relationships of time, reason, contrast, and purpose.

1. Time: when, whenever
2. Reason: because, since
3. Contrast: although, even though, though
4. Purpose: so that

Appendix 6

Transitions

Transitions are words or phrases that show the relationship between two ideas. The most common transitions are used to:

1. Give examples: for example, for instance
2. Add emphasis: in fact, of course
3. Add information: in addition, furthermore, moreover, besides
4. Make comparisons: similarly, likewise
5. Show contrast: however, nevertheless, in contrast, on the contrary, on one/on the other hand
6. Give reasons or results: therefore, as a result, as a consequence, for this/that reason
7. Show sequences: now, then, first (second, etc.) earlier, later, meanwhile, finally

Skills Index

Text Credits

Page 7: "Want to Learn a Language? Don't Make it a Mount Everest" by Tish Durkin, *The New York Times*, September 26, 1992; page 27: "Annapurna: A Woman's Place" by Arlene Blum, 1980, as submitted; page 46: Adapted from "Gender Differences in Communication" by Rose Der at http://www.geocities.com/Wellesley/2052/genddiff.html and "Cross-Gender Communication" by Gladys We; page 62: "Tattoos Across Time and Place" adapted from "Tattoo: Pigments of Imagination" by Cassandra Franklin-Barbajosa, *National Geographic Magazine Online*, December 2004. www.magma.nationalgeographic.com; page 71: Excerpt from "History of Neckwear" by Alan Flusser, from www.neckties.com; page 72: From "2004 Gender Quick Facts: Cosmetic Procedures" by the American Society of Plastic Surgeons, as submitted; page 83: "Socialization and the Life Course" from *Sociology*, ninth edition, and Sociology: *A Brief Introduction*, third edition, by Richard T. Schaefer. © 1992 McGraw-Hill Companies; page 120: "Decision by Consensus" from *The Rising Sun on Main Street, Working with the Japanese*, second edition, by Alison R. Lanier. © 1990 Intercultural Press, Inc.; page 139: "Spray-On Solar-Power Cells Are True Breakthrough" by Stefan Lovgren, *National Geographic News*, January 14, 2005, as submitted. National Geographic Society; page 154: "Themes and Purposes of Art: Art and Nature" from *Gilbert's Living with Art*, sixth edition, by Mark Getlein. © 2002 McGraw-Hill Companies; page 170: Excerpt "Turtle Island" and poem "For the Children" from *Turtle Island* by Gary Snyder. © 1974, New Directions Publishing Group, as submitted.

The publisher apologizes for any apparent infringement of copyright and if notified, will be pleased to rectify any errors or omissions at the earliest opportunity.

Photo Credits

Page 3: © Comstock Images/JupiterImages; 4 (top left): © Jacobs Stock Photography/ Getty Images; 4 (top right): © Ryan McVay/Getty Images; 4 (bottom left): © Patrick Clark/Getty Images; 4 (bottom right): © Mark Thornton/Getty Images; 7: © Jon Burbank/The Image Works; 23: © NASA; 24 (top left): © Bettmann/CORBIS; 24 (top right): © Erling Söderström; 24 (bottom left): © CORBIS SYGMA; 24 (bottom right): AP/Wide World Photos; 27: © Royalty-Free/Corbis Images; 41: © image100/ PunchStock; 45: © Royalty-Free/CORBIS; 46 (top left): © Digital Vision/PunchStock; 46 (top right): © image100/PunchStock; 46 (bottom both): © Royalty-Free/CORBIS; 49 (left): © Ryan McVay/Getty Images; 49 (right): © Andersen Ross/Getty Images; 50: © Stockbyte/PunchStock; 56: © image100 Ltd; 61: © Melba Photo Agency/Alamy; 62 (top left): © Stockbyte/Getty Images; 62 (top right): © Marvin Koner/CORBIS; 62 (bottom both): © Royalty-Free/CORBIS; 64: © Ryan McVay/Getty Images; 81: © Comstock Images/JupiterImages; 82 (top left): © © Creatas; 82 (top right): © BananaStock/ PunchStock; 82 (bottom left): © PhotoDisc; 82 (bottom right): © Don Tremain/Getty Images; 83 (left): © Getty Images; 83 (right): © Ryan McVay/Getty Images; 85: © Patrick Ward/CORBIS; 86: © Alonso Andres R./CORBIS SYGMA; 99: © Richard T. Nowitz/ CORBIS; 100 (left): © Bettmann/CORBIS; 100 (right): The Metropolitan Museum of Art, gift of M. Knowedler & Co.; 102: © CORBIS; 108: © C. Sherburne/PhotoLink/Getty Images; 111: © Harvey Lloyd/Getty Images; 115: © Royalty-Free/CORBIS; 119: © Jose Luis Pelaez/CORBIS; 120 (top left): © Esbin Adnerson/The Image Works; 120 (top right): © Amy C. Etra/The Image Works; 120 (bottom left): © image100/PunchStock; 120 (bottom right): © Jon Burbank/The Image Works; 129: © Digital Vision/Getty Images; 137: © Dynamic Graphics/ JupiterImages; 138 (top left): © Digital Vision/ PunchStock; 138 (top right): © Mark Richards/PhotoEdit; 138 (bottom left): © Warren Gretz/DOE/NREL; 138 (bottom right): © J. Sohm/The Image Works; 153: © PhotoEdit; 154 (top left): © Francis G. Mayer/CORBIS; 154 (top right): © The Newark Museum/Art Resource, NY; 154 (bottom left): © Mark Harmel/Alamy; 154 (bottom right): © Berenice Abbot/Commerce Graphics, Ltd./Courtesy of Joseph Bellows Gallery; 156: © Francis G. Mayer/CORBIS; 157: © Michael S. Yamashita/CORBIS; 158: © Art Resource, NY; 169: © Gary Wagner/Stock Boston; 170 (top left): © Reutres New Media/CORBIS; 170 (top right): © Joel Gordon; 170 (bottom), 171: AP/Wide World Photos; 173: © Royalty-Free/CORBIS; 176: © Manjunath Kiran/ epa/CORBIS; 181: © The Studio Dog/Getty Images.